Do we really need another book of devotional readings? There are a number already available which provide encouragement to our faith. But I know of no other that stimulates biblical thinking as it relates to the needs of the disabled and their caregivers like Dr. Anderson's book, "Forty Days: Finding Refuge in the Ark from the Storms of Disability." Here the disabled will learn of their incredible worth to God and society. Parents with disabled children will find their deepest faith-questions addressed with honesty and sensitivity.

Whether you're dealing with a disability, provide care to such persons, or simply want to examine issues that may challenge your faith, I encourage you to read these devotionals and use the daily reflection questions to go deeper in your faith journey. Here you will learn to read the Bible in a new way by becoming more alert to passages that have direct significance for the disabled and their caregivers. I believe God will meet you in ways that will promote understanding, faith, and a greater love for a Savior who experienced suffering and now offers us His comforting presence and future hope.

Dr. Richard C. Schoenert. Pastor Emeritus, Calvary Church, Roseville, MN. Missionary, One Challenge International.

With years of practical experience in the arena of disability ministry, David Anderson has acquired insights useful to all who will read this God inspired devotional. Like the manna provided by God to Israelites in the wilderness, "Forty Days: Finding Refuge in the Ark from the Storms of Disability" will provide spiritual sustenance sufficient for each day to those living with disability. I highly recommend this for everyone who knows and/or lives with a person experiencing a disabling condition.

Dana Croxton, Founder and President of Enable Ministries.

"Your infant daughter is severely profoundly deaf. Her auditory nerve functions are beyond improvement or repair." That's when reality hit like a hammer blow, and my wife and I knew that our beautiful baby girl would require the deepest measure of our love and devotion as she passed from infancy into adulthood. We were newly married and new Christians, and we immediately turned to God for guidance. However, on an earthly level we had no idea of how to proceed raising a child with a life-long disability, and neither did any of our friends. One thing that would have helped immensely would have been Biblically solid spiritual guidance. I know that had Dr. David Anderson's wonderful book, "Forty Days: Finding Refuge in the Ark from the Storms of Disability" been available, it would have been a daily read of tremendous blessing to us. If you or someone you love is the parent or caregiver of a person with disability I strongly encourage you to get it, read it, and be tremendously blessed!

Dennis D. Frey, Th.D., President, Master's International University of Divinity

FORTY DAYS

Finding Refuge in the Ark
from the Storms of Disability

David W Anderson

WESTBOW
PRESS®
A DIVISION OF THOMAS NELSON
& ZONDERVAN

WestBow Press books may be ordered through booksellers or by contacting:

WestBow Press
A Division of Thomas Nelson & Zondervan
1663 Liberty Drive
Bloomington, IN 47403
www.westbowpress.com
1 (866) 928-1240

ISBN: 978-1-9736-2488-2 (sc)
ISBN: 978-1-9736-2487-5 (e)

Library of Congress Control Number: 2018904123

Print information available on the last page.

The cover illustration is original art work done by Ukrainian artist, Anastasia Taran (anastasiataran.jimbo.com). Used by permission of the artist.

Crossing Bridges, Inc., is an independent, non-governmental, inter-denominational, and nonprofit organization established in 2005 with a mission is to bring light and hope to people with disabilities and their families, around the world. Crossing Bridges partners with individuals, families, churches, schools, and other organizations to promote awareness of, and responsiveness to, the needs and abilities of persons facing disabling conditions. We seek to encourage and empower persons dealing with disability — and those who serve them — to bring about changed lives and changed societies. Our goal is to be a catalyst for reconciliation, social justice, and church outreach.

WestBow Press rev. date: 4/24/2018

ACKNOWLEDGMENTS

Other than God, the person who must be acknowledged is my wife, Florence, who has been my life- and ministry-companion for more than 53 years. She also served as critic and proofreader for this devotional book. Thanks also to Anastasia Taran for sharing her artistic talent by creating the illustration for the cover of the book.

The individuals referred to in these devotionals are people with whom I have ministered over the years. Some names have been changed to accommodate anonymity. I am grateful to God for brining me into contact with these people who have shared their lives and experience with me over the years. In many ways they are among my greatest teachers.

Most of all, I want to acknowledge God for his grace expressed to me in various ways each day. The journey he has taken me on as a husband, father, special education teacher, university professor, adult Bible fellowship leader, missionary-teacher, and author has been fascinating and has helped me more fully grasp who he is and who I am as his child and servant.

PREFACE

Just over 50 years ago, God brought me into the field of disability studies and special education, but not through personal connection with someone who had a disability. Shortly after graduating from college with a major in Bible, God planted in my mind the idea of becoming a teacher. I had begun taking evening courses at a local university while continuing to work in a soils lab. A Christian acquaintance from the business office of the company for which I worked, perhaps aware that I was thinking about becoming a teacher, was led by God to share a copy of a magazine with me, in which there was an article about brain chemistry and Down syndrome. I remember little of that article, but I clearly recall the accompanying photograph of a beautiful six-year-old girl with Down syndrome. God used that photograph to arouse in me an interest in special education. Since that beginning, God has given me the privilege of teaching children with various disabilities, training others to become special education teachers, and working with pastors and seminaries to promote the importance of active ministry to and with individuals and families affected by disability.

The ensuing relationships with individuals and families who deal with disabilities, particularly in Africa and Eastern Europe, has given me insight into the struggles that they experience — struggles which may be only slightly easier in the U.S. because of social and educational policies. These devotionals are the outcome of my relationships with these various individuals and families. The concerns addressed in these devotional studies are common to all families that deal with disabilities. It is my prayer that these devotional studies will draw these families and individuals into a deeper relationship with God.

The topics addressed in these devotionals, however, are not just important for families directly impacted by disability, partly because if we live long enough there is a good possibility that we might find ourselves disabled in some way, if only because of age. But most churches and seminaries fail to consider disability as an area of spiritual need. These devotional thoughts will be helpful to pastors, missionaries, and Christian education workers who need to understand or discover ways by which to minister to people affected by disability. The impact of disability is felt by the entire family, requiring the church to be sensitive to the whole family's needs.

DAY 1

TIME FOR DANCING

"The joy of our hearts has ceased; our dancing has been turned to mourning." (Lamentations 5:15)

"You have turned for me my mourning into dancing; you have loosed my sackcloth and clothed me with gladness." (Psalm 30:11)

"Let them praise his name with dancing, making melody to him with tambourine and lyre!" (Psalm 149:3)

"Then shall the young women rejoice in the dance, and the young men and the old shall be merry. I will turn their mourning into joy; I will comfort them, and give them gladness for sorrow." (Jeremiah 31:13)

The illustration on the cover of this book was drawn by Anastasia, a young artist living in Ukraine. Anastasia's artistic gift is obvious to all who see her creations. But what they do not see from her paintings, is that Anastasia is a person with a physical disability, possibly as a result of having contracted polio as a child. She is a wheelchair user and has limited use of her hands. It is not uncommon for people, when they see someone with an obvious disability, to see the limitations but miss the person — often, in their mind, assuming the person is more disabled than he or she really is.

The illustration shows a young girl sitting in her wheelchair practicing ballet movements, but seeing herself in the mirror standing. Some might see the illustration as indication of Anastasia's discomfort or sadness about being restricted to a wheelchair, and her desire to be like other young women who live without a physical impairment. But they would be wrong!

Anastasia is quite comfortable with who she is as a child of the King. What the illustration is meant to convey is that though her body is disabled, her spirit — her true self — is not bound. She does not see herself as a disabled person, but as a person living with a disability. The disability does not define her, nor does it limit her ability to "dance" before the Lord.

Shock, confusion, depression, and anger frequently follow receiving the news that your child or other loved one has a disability. Your emotional state when hearing this may be similar to what Jeremiah expressed in Lamentations 5:15 — your joy has ended and your dancing has turned to mourning. Friends and extended family may attempt to be supportive and offer encouraging words, but their thoughts may fall on deaf ears as the tyranny of the unknown settles into your heart and mind. But in reality, even those who are not disabled face a future of possibilities which can be positive or negative. We generally do not dwell on the negative possibilities, as if positive thinking will disallow the negative, but disability can happen to anyone at any time; it neither asks nor needs our approval. Thus, the lack of joy and hyper-concern about the future for the one who is disabled and for the rest of the family, settles into our thinking.

But this is because we have taken our eyes off God and focus too strongly on the condition and circumstances of disability. Even Jeremiah countered his words of lament by relating God's promise to turn mourning into joy, to give comfort and gladness (Jeremiah 31:13). The dancing, merriment, comfort, joy and gladness, mentioned in Psalms 30 and 149 do not just focus on eternity. Having a disability, even a severe disability, does not prohibit a person or family from rejoicing and dancing before the Lord. Anastasia is but one example of a person who is joy-full, whose spirit dances in worship. Having discovered the artistic gift God has given her, she uses that gift to bless others. The motto on her website is "I draw positive." I would say Anastasia also *lives* positive. Through her paintings, her photography, and her smile, Anastasia communicates joy and happiness to others, and blesses those who take the time to know *her*, not just her physical limitation.

FOR REFLECTION

What do you see when your look at your child or loved one who is challenged by a disability? Meeting the physical, medical, emotional needs of that person can quickly drain your energy, and can sometimes consume your thoughts. What gifts might you miss in the busyness of life with your child or loved one? How has your disabled family member been a gift *to you?* Do you need to alter your perspective from needs to blessings? What do you need to do so that God can turn your mourning into joy (Jeremiah 31:13)? How can you and your loved one, even if sitting in a wheelchair, dance and make melody in praise to God?

DAY 2

LOOKING FOR ANSWERS: A GOOD AND PERFECT GIFT?

*"Behold, children are a heritage from the LORD,
the fruit of the womb a reward." (Psalm 127:3)*

*"Every good gift and every perfect gift is from above,
coming down from the Father of lights with whom there
is no variation or shadow due to change." (James 1:17)*

As an experienced special education teacher, and a trainer of others who desire to work with children with special needs, Mary thought she knew everything about Down syndrome, a genetic condition which can result in physical problems, developmental delays, and cognitive impairment. That is, until prenatal screening indicated the unborn child she was carrying would be born with Down syndrome. Hearing this brought shock, as it would to any expectant mom. Her faith was challenged as she, like most women in this situation, wondered "why?" But Mary's faith was stretched and deepened as she trusted God, knowing that God remains loving and good and would walk with her in this new adventure.

Perhaps you find yourself in a similar situation, having a child with a disabling condition. No one is prepared to face the challenges this may bring: the "death" of the ideal child, learning how to meet your child's special needs, sensing or imagining negative reactions from others, and the nagging questions about God's love and faithfulness.

You may wonder how a child born with a disabling condition can be a "heritage" from the Lord as the psalmist said, or a "good and perfect gift" from God as James wrote. Questions may circle through your mind: Where was God when my child was developing in utero? Did God made a mistake? Since every good and perfect gift comes from the Father, did this child who, in the eyes of the world, is less than perfect come from Satan? But your struggle to discover meaning in your situation and find an answer to the question "Why?" may go unanswered.

If this is, or has been your experience, you are not alone. It is a common reaction for all parents who have given birth to a child with a disability, and shared by parents who have a family member that has become disabled through illness or injury. Your search for answers is not simply an emotional quest, it is a spiritual search for understanding. You believe you are part of the family of God, but at the same time culture (and sometimes the church) wrongly attributes the child's disability to punishment for unconfessed sin or a broken taboo. This focus, however, tends to be centered solely on yourself, your child, your situation, and all of the unknowns of the future. "Where was God?" many not be the right question. Perhaps you need to ask, "Where am I in my faith?"

Mary pondered whether to ask God to reconstruct the chromosomal structure of each cell in her unborn child's body, or to simply trust God to give her a heart of love for her child. As she wrestled with these ideas, God helped Mary grow in her assurance of his ongoing love, goodness, and presence despite how her life would be altered as the mother of a child with Down syndrome. The doctor's diagnosis was accurate, Mary's son does have Down syndrome. It would deny reality to say that there have not been challenges at times, but her son is a loving boy and a welcome part of her family.

FOR REFLECTION

Remember how deeply God loves you and your child *just as you are*. God's love is a practical and empowering reality. Though earthly relationships change, God's love and character do not (Numbers 23:19).

Proverbs 3:5 says trust in the Lord. If you have a child who is disabled it is sometimes hard to know where God is leading. Trust God and be open to learning new skills and values through the gift of your child.

TAKE ACTION

Meditate on 1 John 4:16. God's love is not dependent on our circumstances or our understanding of what God is doing in our lives. Embrace your child and trust God's wisdom. Consider how you can show God's love to your child — and how your child can help you understand God's love.

DAY 3

DESPAIR, OR HOPE IN THE LORD

"But this I call to mind, and therefore I have hope: The steadfast love of the LORD never ceases; his mercies never come to an end; they are new every morning; great is your faithfulness. 'The LORD is my portion,' says my soul, 'therefore I will hope in him.'" (Lamentations 3:21-24)

Mama B is the mother of two boys who have muscular dystrophy. The older brother requires the use of a wheelchair, and the younger brother has begun to show increased muscle weakness which affects his gait. Abandoned by her husband and ostracized by her extended family and community, Mama B struggles to raise her sons alone. Even her church makes her feel unwelcome.

In the depths of despair, Mama B had reached the point where she considered killing her sons and ending her own life. But this thought weighed heavily on her heart, creating guilt which deepened her emotional brokenness. Feeling alone and stigmatized, Mama B would avoid making eye contact with others, and would barely speak to strangers. Though a believer, she experienced much stress and discouragement, feeling that God had also abandoned her.

Mama B is not the only mother of a child with a disability who has felt this loneliness and hopelessness. Perhaps as the parent of a child with a disability you have also felt great emotional and spiritual distress.

In Lamentations 3:1–20, Jeremiah described his situation using terms with which Mama B and others in her situation can easily relate. Jeremiah spoke of being under the rod of God's wrath ... driven into darkness ... having God's hand turned against him ... besieged with bitterness and hardship ... dwelling in darkness from which he cannot escape (vv. 1–7). He believed his cries for help were not heard by God because he has shut out his prayers (v. 8). He feels torn to pieces (v. 11), and believes himself to be the laughingstock of the people, who taunt him daily (v. 14). His soul knows no peace and he has forgotten what happiness is (v. 17). His ability to endure has weakened, as has his hope from the Lord (v. 18).

Perhaps you share Jeremiah's lament as you deal with disability in your family. Caring for your disabled child may seem empty and fruitless, with any change or growth slow or limited. Dwelling on this leads to deep sorrow of the soul.

It is important to continue reading verses 21–26 in Lamentations 3, which show a radical change in Jeremiah's emotional state. What caused his complete U-turn in his thinking? He remembered that the steadfast love of the LORD never ceases, that God's mercies are new each day, and recognized the greatness of God's faithfulness.

As Mama B came to better understand God's love for her and her children *just the way they are,* her demeanor — her whole life — dramatically changed, just as did Jeremiah's. Change also came from realizing she was not alone in her distress. Along with knowing God's presence, she also bonded with other mothers in a similar situation. She is now able to laugh and smile brightly, joyfully engaging in conversation with others. She no longer feels alone and discouraged, having established a close fellowship with other families who deal with disability. Her relationship with her Lord has deepened, and she openly shares with others the assurance she has gained about God's love for her and her children.

If you are plagued with discouragement and despair, you can also have this change of heart as you meditate on God's ongoing goodness.

FOR REFLECTION

Why is our attention drawn to the difficulties faced in life, but we quickly forget the blessings from God we have received? How can you adjust your focus even in the midst of struggles?

Read the Gospel of Luke and note Jesus' demonstration of compassion to people oppressed by the community because of disability or disease.

TAKE ACTION

Spend time searching the Scriptures to learn more about God's goodness and steadfast love. Find other families with whom you can be a source of mutual support and encouragement.

DAY 4

YOU ARE NOT ALONE

"Go therefore and make disciples of all nations, baptizing them in the name of the Father and of the Son and of the Holy Spirit, teaching them to observe all that I have commanded you. And behold, I am with you always, to the end of the age." (Matthew 28:19-20)

Caring for the needs of a child who has a disability can sometimes feel like a lonely job. Facing the same struggles each day but perhaps seeing little progress, and finding time for other necessary chores around the house can exhaust your physical, emotional, and spiritual energy. Sometimes parents can feel lost and alone as they strive to do all that is required to meet the child's needs and promote his or her development. Certain ages or stages of growth can be more challenging to both a parent and the child. Though all children pass through the same stages, for a child who has a disability, these stages are often delayed or prolonged.

Today's scripture is Jesus' "Great Commission" in which he assigns to all believers the task of proclaiming the gospel to all people groups. Usually, this passage is used to emphasize making disciples through evangelism or missionary activity. But it also relates to parenting a child with a disability. The phrase "all nations" does not refer to countries, as we understand nations today. It signifies "all people groups," including people with disabilities. If your child has a physical, cognitive, or emotional disability, no matter how severe, your mission field is in your home. Your responsibility is to faithfully disciple your child, modeling Jesus' love and compassion. Your child's ability to understand or to respond is not your concern; you simply act as Jesus would. You "be" Jesus to your child.

But the last part of Jesus' instructions is equally important, though it often receives less emphasis. Jesus' promise is especially meaningful to parents of children with a disability who feel stressed by trying to meet the child's and the family's needs each day. Jesus says, *"and behold,"* which calls attention to the importance of what he is about to say: "you can be certain of my presence." Jesus promises never to leave our side as we go about the task of making disciples. His abiding presence brings comfort in a world that often seems chaotic or grossly unpredictable to families affected by disability. Jesus is at your side as you care for your disabled child.

Jesus' promise echoes the message given by the angel to Joseph regarding the baby to be born: "they shall call his name Immanuel, which means God with us" (Matthew 1:23). He assures us, as his followers, that although he will no longer be with us in bodily form, he is still "with us" to guide, assist, protect, uphold, and bless. There are no conditions we must meet; no circumstances that lead to his absence. Not even our own disability or the persistent, often stressful calling to care for a disabled child.

FOR REFLECTION

In Zechariah 4:10, God promises that the new temple being built in Jerusalem will be finished, and people who "despised the day of small things (small beginnings) shall rejoice" at its completion. Relating this thought to raising a child with a disability, "small things" includes the seemingly insignificant or unimportant things about your child that go unrecognized because of your busyness, like subtle changes in your child's ability or behavior. How much time do you take to enjoy those small changes? You may even miss the joy your child is, and brings to the family. Take time to recognize and celebrate your child's "un-special" needs. Remember, those "things" are small, but God is great.

The stress of meeting the needs of a child with disability can be overwhelming and seem unending. Remembering Jesus' promise always be with you can help you to relax and release that stress. What can you do each day to remind yourself of his presence?

TAKE ACTION

Time spent caring for a child who has significant disabilities can interfere with relationships with friends. How can you prevent this from happening? Who can help you maintain a proper focus?

DAY 5

DECEIVING APPEARANCES: BEAUTY OF THE DISABLED

"Do not look on his appearance or on the height of his stature, because I have rejected him. For the LORD sees not as man sees: man looks on the outward appearance, but the LORD looks on the heart." (1 Samuel 16:7)

People often hold stereotypical notions about disability, assuming someone who is severely disabled has little to offer, and perhaps repulsed by their physical appearance. Such responses can even be evident within the Christian community. But people who feel this way fail to acknowledge the inherent worth of every person, able-bodied or disabled, as created in the image of God.

In the familiar story of Beauty and the Beast, a handsome prince is transformed into a hideous beast, his true identity lying hidden beneath his outward appearance. Only the love of a beautiful maiden will allow him to revert to his former handsomeness. To save her father from death, Belle agrees to remain at the palace of the Beast. Over a period of time, she comes to know and care for the Beast despite his physical unattractiveness and confesses her love for him. She learns that seeing beauty is a matter of the heart, not the eyes.

Life is not a fairy tale, but the message of this story is important. The heart allows us to see beneath the outward appearance of a person, and to see the ugliness of our misjudging others. Sarah is a teenage girl with a significant cognitive disability and some minor physical difficulties. She is unable to speak and we cannot be sure how much she understands what she hears. Some people turn away rather than interact with Sarah in any way. But that is to their loss.

Sarah has a beauty that shines from within. When worship music begins, Sarah "leads" us in worship with her whole body. She moves to the front of the church and "dances" before the Lord, swaying to the music. Her hands point toward heaven, and her face glows with joy. My eyes tear up watching the pure honesty of her worship, which surely brings a smile to Jesus' face. There is no hesitation in offering herself to the Lord. She helps people who are able-bodied recognize that we are all dependent on God who is able.

As dignity and value are not dependent on what we can accomplish, so beauty is not dependent on appearance. Dignity, value, and beauty are attributes bestowed by God, in whose image we are created. They cannot be lost through congenital or acquired disability. Sarah helps us learn what God told Samuel: to look beneath the "mask" of an unconventional mind or body to see the beauty of the person.

We need to see persons with disabilities as God does: possessing worth and value equal to that of able-bodied persons. We need to see them with love and compassion as Jesus did. That God designs disability into a person or allows a person to become disabled for purposes beyond our understanding strongly indicates that God sees beauty and potential even in the most severely disabled. If we fail to see the beauty of the disabled, might we not also fail to see the beauty of God?

FOR REFLECTION

To see their beauty calls for humility such as Paul commands in Philippians 2:2–4. What might God want you to learn from your child who is disabled?

Sometimes caring for a disabled child and dealing with the thoughts and attitudes of others drains our energy reserve. What does it take for you to remain focused on your child's beauty rather than just his or her needs?

TAKE ACTION

Paul's admonishment in Romans 12:2 is that we not be conformed to this world, but transformed by the renewal of our mind. This includes transformation in our understanding of disability and beauty, in how you see your disabled loved one. What is beautiful about your child? List what is beautiful about your child and the blessings this child brings to your life, and give thanks to God for his gift.

DAY 6

WHO SINNED, THIS MAN OR HIS PARENTS?

"As he passed by, (Jesus) saw a man blind from birth. And his disciples asked him, 'Rabbi, who sinned, this man or his parents, that he was born blind?' Jesus answered, 'It was not that this man sinned, or his parents, but that the works of God might be displayed in him.'" (John 9:1-3)

The disciples' question is not unusual. Many think of disability the way the disciples did, and assume disability is a result of personal sin, either of the person who is disabled or of his parents. Disabilities result from many things, including genetic abnormalities, accidental injuries, illness, and aging. But God's punishment for sin is not a reason someone is born with or acquires a disability. If this was the case, everyone would be disabled, since everyone has sinned (Romans 3:23).

We like to assume we have control over what happens in life and search for an explanation when something unexpected occurs. Hence, the disciples asked Jesus "why?"— just as people do today when someone is born with an impairment or becomes disabled. If Jesus mentioned a particular sin as the reason for the man's blindness, the disciples, who were obviously not disabled, could feel self-justified. Their question was not motivated by compassion for the man, but by curiosity about sin. The man was merely a subject for theological discussion. Jesus' answer challenged their thinking by focusing not on a reason, but a *purpose* for his blindness: "that the works of God may be displayed in him." Jesus made it clear that the man's blindness was unrelated to sin, thereby altering the way they saw the man from sinner to someone through whom God can be glorified. People knew the man simply as "a man blind from birth." But from God's perspective, his disability was not his identity.

God still works in unanticipated ways and through unexpected people. Upon meeting someone with a severe disability, people generally see weakness and inability. They see what is to them imperfection and overlook the possibility that God can work in and through the person; disability is not an obstacle for God. Even parents of a child who is disabled can be as short-sighted as the disciples.

The man has been blind since birth. We do not know his age, but certainly many were aware of his presence yet failed to show compassion as Jesus did toward all he met who were oppressed in some manner. The disciples saw him as an unsolved riddle of suffering rather than a person with a need. Jesus cured the man of his blindness, but that was not the work of God Jesus referred to. Jesus said the man was born blind so that the works of God might be displayed in _him,_ not in his being cured. God worked in the man's heart so that he later confessed belief in Jesus and worshiped him (John 9:23).

The man's blindness gave opportunity for Jesus to show God's love. But demonstrating God's love does not necessitate a cure of disability. God's work in the heart is what is crucial. Being disabled does not prevent a person from glorifying God through actions or testimony. Many people who are disabled give strong witness of God's love and grace.

FOR REFLECTION

Jesus said "*we* must work the works of him who sent me" (John 9:4). We all have a role to play in Jesus' ministry today, whether able-bodied or disabled. As God placed this blind man in the path of the disciples, so he has placed your disabled child in your "path." Consider what role you play in working the works of God, and how you can help equip your son or daughter to do works that will bring glory to God.

The once-blind man's gaining sight is minor compared to the healing of his relationship with God. Jesus wants that same transformation in people today. By what words and actions can you share the good news with your child?

TAKE ACTION

List ways God has worked through your child to bring glory to himself.

DAY 7

FEARFULLY AND WONDERFULLY MADE

"You formed my inward parts; you knitted me together in my mother's womb. I praise you, for I am fearfully and wonderfully made. Wonderful are your works; my soul knows it very well. My frame was not hidden from you, when I was being made in secret, intricately woven in the depths of the earth." (Psalm 139:13-14)

David's words in Psalm 139 masterfully depict God's involvement in the creation of each individual. He pictures God as having personally knit together in the womb each person according to his design, including our physicality and abilities. To say we are "fearfully and wonderfully made" captures the awesomeness and distinctiveness of humankind as the highest of God's created beings. We are each individually pieced together according to God's intent.

Parents of a child born with a mental or physical impairment might ask whether this teaching applies to their child. Could God have made a mistake? Did God lose control? My mother would knit sweaters while watching television. Occasionally she would say "I dropped a stitch," and undo some of her work to be redone. Could God have "dropped a stitch" in knitting a child together in the womb?

The psalmist does not directly answer these questions, but we have no reason to assume that God was not involved or lost control when "knitting together" a child born with a disability. Many disabling conditions are the result of living in a fallen, sinful world, but this does not mean God has no control over certain events. David's words allow that congenital impairments may be part of God's design, for reasons known only to God. And his words affirm that our design comes from God's loving heart, with our best interest and his own glory in mind in our "fashioning." Exactly how God is involved or why he does not intervene in a child's embryonic or fetal development to prevent or correct a genetic problem we are not told. But any notion that God made a mistake brings his sovereignty and wisdom into question and must be dismissed. Also to be rejected is the idea that disability is punishment for sin.

The fact that our understanding is limited may lead us to question God's goodness and love. Having been individually designed by God means God sees beauty, potential, and value, even in people who have a severe disability. They are equally his by creation, and are equally loved, just the way they are. God's desire is to make himself known through individuals and families. We must seek to understand what he is revealing through each person, able-bodied or disabled. God wants to use each family member to bless others (Ephesians 2:10). Our disability is not stronger than God's ability!

Sheila is in her late 20s and has a moderate intellectual disabled because of Down syndrome. We first met when Sheila was a student in a special education school in Kenya. She has probably gained as much formal education as she is able to attain, but Sheila continues to be associated with that school. Having developed the necessary skills, Sheila now serves as a helper for the younger children. Socially, she is comfortable conversing with non-disabled adults and finds pleasure in serving others. We celebrate with her God's gift of compassion. Her life shows purpose and value that her parents may not have seen when she was a young child. The attitude of her heart is an unexpected blessing.

FOR REFLECTION

Disability can lead to questioning God's love and wisdom. Romans 8:28 gives assurance that what happens in your life, or the life of your disabled family member, is directed toward your good and God's glory — despite our inability to comprehend God's actions.

Psalm 100:5 says God is good and his love and faithfulness endure. This being true, can being disabled prevent us from being "more than conquerors" (Romans 8:35–37)? Consider how disability can be a gift from God because he loves us and knows it can result in our spiritual growth, making us the kind of person he wants us to be.

TAKE ACTION

Pray that God would help you to trust his sovereignty.

DAY 8

WHO IS GREATEST IN THE KINGDOM OF HEAVEN?

"Truly, I say to you, unless you turn and become like children, you will never enter the kingdom of heaven. Whoever humbles himself like this child is the greatest in the kingdom of heaven." (Matthew 18:3–4)

Proud of their association with Jesus, the disciples asked him which of them would be the greatest in the kingdom of heaven. They assumed that Jesus' kingdom would be patterned after familiar earthly realms, and they would be given important positions. Their focus was on organization and status within the kingdom. Jesus' answer focused on the characteristics of those who enter the kingdom. He gave them a visual answer to make his point. Placing a young child in their midst (Mark 9:36 adds that Jesus took the child in his arms). Jesus explained that those who humble themselves like this child would be the greatest.

Making a child the center of attention probably shocked his disciples because little children were not regarded as important in Jesus' day, and because they expected him to identify one of them as most important. Instead, Jesus' action and teaching centered on the "littleness" of a child, who is dependent on the good will of his parents. The contrast between Jesus' words and worldly views of ambition and importance could not be more explicit. Jesus makes humility the focus: at the center of kingdom life are those who come to Christ with the openness, sincerity, trust, and vulnerability as evident in young children. If Jesus were asked this question today, I suspect he might use a child with a disability as his example.

As the parent of a child with a significant disability, perhaps you have sensed negative attitudes from people who wonder why you care about the child, why you did not give the child up for adoption or, if the disability was identified prior to birth, why you did not abort the baby. They may hide these feeling behind comments like "You must be so special," or voice admiration for your "sacrifice," while silently questioning the wisdom of your action.

It is important to recognize that weakness and vulnerability are not necessarily negative or purposeless. In our weakness, limitation, and vulnerability we most clearly experience God's strength. When God looks at someone who is disabled, he does not see weakness, inability, or a person of limited value. He sees someone made in his image and through whom he can display his greatness. When viewed as a gift from a loving God, vulnerability connects us with Christ, who made himself vulnerable by laying aside his right to experience the glory and majesty of the Godhead through his incarnation.

When we rely on God's strength and place ourselves in the hands of the Master, offering our weakness or limitation to God, God is able to bring glory to himself and accomplish greater things than ever imagined. We who are able-bodied have a lot to learn from our children or friends who have a disability, who often more easily display humility than we who are able-bodied.

FOR REFLECTION

Becoming like a little child means relinquishing attitudes of self-importance or prideful ambition and recognizing our dependence on God. Are you more like the disciples, seeking positions of importance, or are you like a little child?

The kingdom belongs to those who receive it as a gift, without presumption of deserving God's grace and mercy. People with disabilities may appreciate this gift more than people who are able-bodied. How do Jesus' words in Matthew 19:30 and Matthew 20:16 add to what he told his disciples about greatness and humbleness?

The disciples were slow to understand Jesus' message in Matthew 18. In Matthew 19:13–15, people bring their children to Jesus for him to lay hands on and pray for the children, but the disciples want him to send them away. Jesus has to remind the disciples: "Let the little children come to me and do not hinder them, for to such belongs the kingdom of heaven." In what ways are you "bringing" your child to Jesus?

TAKE ACTION

Meditate on Paul's teaching in Philippians 2:5–8 about having a humble attitude like that of Jesus.

DAY 9

THE HEART OF A GIFTED LEADER

"As each has received a gift, use it to serve one another, as good stewards of God's varied grace: whoever speaks, as one who speaks oracles of God; whoever serves, as one who serves by the strength that God supplies—in order that in everything God may be glorified through Jesus Christ." (1 Peter 4:10-11)

Does "each has received a gift" include children who are mentally or physically disabled? Are these children equipped to serve others as a good steward of God's grace? Can God be glorified through a child with severe mental or physical disabilities? If you have a child or a family member who is disabled, these are questions that you (or they) may ponder.

Many people might believe the answer to these questions is "no," considering the person with the disability unimportant and unable to serve others or to bring honor to God. But they would be wrong in that conclusion. Even parents of a child with mental or physical disabilities may become caught up in the busyness of meeting their child's special needs and making it through another day. They might miss seeing the "specialness" of the child God has graced them with, and the opportunity to see God's love in their son or daughter. Given the sometimes heavy demands of caring for a child who is significantly disabled, parents may neglect to intentionally share God's love with the child. Perhaps, because of your situation, you can relate to this.

Elliot is a young boy whom God has used to bless me and others.

Elliot was born with cerebral palsy. Because of damage to the motor control centers in his brain which occurred prior to or during birth, Elliot's muscles are tight, making his movements spastic (jerky) and uncontrolled. With the aid of a walker he can make his way around his limited environment, but his movements are awkward. The paralysis also affects his tongue movements, making it impossible for him to speak. But Elliot is intelligent, able to understand and to learn, and he is very enthusiastic about life. His smile, which lights up his entire face, conveys love and acceptance of others, including both other children who have a disability and people who are able-bodied.

More importantly, Elliot loves the Lord. He readily joins in during times of praise and worship, moving to the music while holding his walker for support. When he "sings" and "prays" aloud, he uses a language only the Holy Spirit can understand. Although I cannot understand the language of his grunts and utterances, to God's ears it is the sweet sound of praise.

Elliot is a gifted worship leader and draws others into worshiping with him. John 1:6–9 describes John the Baptist as a man sent from God to bear witness to the Light that is Jesus. The same can be said of Elliot; *he* is not the light, but his life points others to that Light. Does Elliot have a sense of being called by God? Perhaps not, but he does bring glory to his heavenly Father through his passion, his enthusiasm for life, his outgoing personality, his eagerness and courage to try new things, and through his worship. For me, Elliot is a more effective worship leader than the praise and worship bands we often see at church!

Jesus' disciples asked, "Who is the greatest in the kingdom of heaven?" My answer would be, those who, like Elliot, receive the gift of salvation, receive God's love, openly and without presumption, and use their ability to point others to the Lord.

FOR REFLECTION

As the parent of a child with a disability, step back from the daily responsibilities of meeting his or her needs. Look closely at your child to see how God is revealed to you through him or her. How does your child lead you to a deeper worship of God?

TAKE ACTION

What understanding of God do you hope your child receives through your caring for his or her special needs? What specific things can you do to "show" God to your child? Write a list of specific things and pray for God's strength to do them.

DAY 10

AM I UP TO THE TASK? SEEING YOURSELF AS GOD DOES

"The angel of the LORD appeared to (Gideon) and said to him, 'The LORD is with you, O mighty man of valor . . . . Go in this might of yours and save Israel from the hand of Midian; do not I send you?' (Gideon) said to him, 'Please, Lord, how can I save Israel? Behold, my clan is the weakest in Manasseh, and I am the least in my father's house.'" (Judges 6:12, 14–15)

Gideon was secretly threshing wheat in a winepress in order to hide his actions from Israel's enemies who would steal the wheat. As he was busily threshing wheat, he received a call from the angel of the Lord, who addressed him as "a mighty man of valor." Gideon's commission was to deliver the Israelites from their enemies. But Gideon's perception of himself differed from God's. The angel of the LORD called him a mighty warrior, a courageous hero. But Gideon, not a man of strong faith or courage, disagreed, arguing that his family is the least in the tribe of Manasseh, and he is the youngest — the weakest or least significant — in his family. In other words, he does not feel up to the task; God should choose another.

Perhaps as the parent of a child with disabilities, you also feel "weak," not up to the task. Parenting a child who has a physical or mental disability presents challenges which can exhaust your physical, emotional, and spiritual strength, challenges that are not likely to lessen significantly over time. Imagine yourself busily changing the diaper of a six year old child with a severe disability, or struggling to position him properly so you can feed him. If, in the midst of this activity, God greeted you as a valiant warrior, how would you respond? Would you echo Gideon's claim of weakness and inability? Gideon asked, "If God is with us, why have we experienced such difficulty? Has the Lord forsaken us?" (v. 13). Have you also felt forsaken as you raise your disabled child? Gideon saw himself as too weak and insignificant to lead Israel against their enemies.

If this is your experience, you are not alone; most parents facing these challenges on a daily basis feel this way at times. These questions have probably come into your heart and mind more than once. Perhaps you may wonder, "Where are God's promises?" or "Why does God not perform a miracle and cure my child of disability?" Perhaps you feel confused and helpless when facing the issues of raising a child with a disability, a disability which will present on-going problems for your child and for you. Maybe you do not see yourself as a "mighty warrior," and ask "does God care?"

But you are not alone. God is with you. He knows what you are going through. Gideon was given a sign to affirm God's presence (Judges 6:19–24). God may not give you such a sign, but his promise to Gideon — "I will be with you" (Judges 6:17) — is his promise to you, too. And with his presence, comes his strength, enabling you to raise your child well, to be the person of valor he has designed you to be.

FOR REFLECTION

Paul says we are God's workmanship, or masterpiece, created in Christ Jesus to do good works which God prepared beforehand for us to do (Ephesians 2:10, NIV). How does this apply to your "good work" as the parent of a child with a disability? Do you see your disabled child a "masterpiece" created by God? (See also Psalms 127:3 and 139:13–16.)

TAKE ACTION

Do you see yourself as weak, or do you see yourself as God saw Gideon, a mighty hero? Read Gideon's full story (Judges 6–9) and note how his faith grew as he acted in obedience. Allow God's promise and presence in Gideon's life to encourage you as you face various struggles raising your disabled child. List ways in which God has shown himself to be present in your battles, and give him thanks.

DAY 11

TO REBEL OR TO TRUST? OVERCOMING THROUGH DISABILITY

"Jacob was left alone. And a man wrestled with him until the breaking of the day. When the man saw that he did not prevail against Jacob, he touched his hip socket, and Jacob's hip was put out of joint as he wrestled with him . . . . Jacob said, 'I will not let you go unless you bless me.' . . . . And he said, 'Your name shall no longer be called Jacob, but Israel, for you have striven with God and with men, and have prevailed.' " (Genesis 32:24-28)

People struggle against God for many reasons. If you or a family member has a disability you have probably fought with God, trying to understand why he allowed the disability to "invade" your life, over which you assumed you had full control. Or perhaps you wrestled in prayer seeking a cure. When God did not respond to your wishes, you had a choice to rebel against God or to place your trust in God. The story of Jacob helps us understand that God's way is best, and often includes hidden surprises.

Jacob was one of the major patriarchs of Israel, the father of 12 sons from whom the tribes of Israel descended. But Jacob's biography does not present him in a positive light. His name means "deceiver," an appropriate description given that he managed to steal the birthright from his older fraternal twin brother, and later deceived his elderly and blind father into giving him the paternal blessing that would have gone to Esau. Jacob was not alone in this trickery; his mother,

Rebekah, instigated his deception (see Genesis 27). However, God used their duplicity to bring about what he had revealed before the twins were born: the elder shall serve the younger (Genesis 25:23).

Knowing that Esau would be furious, Jacob quickly fled from home after receiving the blessing. By the time we get to Genesis 32, about 20 years have passed and Jacob is returning home with his family, servants, and livestock. When learning that Esau was coming to meet him, Jacob became concerned for his family's safety and sent them to a safe location while he spent the night alone.

During the night, Jacob was visited by a "man" who wrestled with him until dawn. Jacob prevailed until the visitor dislocated Jacob's hip, leaving him with a permanent disability. Despite being seriously injured, Jacob was able to cling to his opponent, and said he would not release his grip until he received a blessing from the "man." In response, Jacob's name was changed to *Israel*, meaning "he who strives with God."

Though Jacob ultimately lost the match, he won a victory. God's gift of a disability helped him recognize his dependence upon God rather than focusing on himself and doing things his way. Realizing it was God he struggled with, Jacob said "I have seen God face to face, yet my life has been spared" (Genesis 32:30).

The blessing of a disability made Jacob understand he could not truly overcome his opponent. His new name signified a changed life — no longer was he the schemer and deceiver. The fullness of God's blessing included permanent disability, which would be a continual reminder of God's grace. Could it be that your vision needs to change so that you see disability as a gift, rather than a curse?

FOR REFLECTION

Carefully read Genesis 32:24–32. Reflect on how Jacob's disability was an act of grace which enabled him to escape the reality of who he had been. Does this change your view of disability?

Consider how spiritual blessing and physical affliction can complement one another and draw us closer to God.

TAKE ACTION

Do you know someone who is personally dealing with disability or has a family member who is or became disabled that you can encourage by sharing Jacob's story?

DAY 12

DO WE SEE POSSIBILITIES OR DISABILITIES? ATTITUDES MATTER!

"Rejoice in the Lord always ... do not be anxious about anything, but in everything by prayer and supplication with thanksgiving let your requests be made known to God. And the peace of God, which surpasses all understanding, will guard your hearts and your minds in Christ Jesus ... whatever is true, whatever is honorable, whatever is just, whatever is pure, whatever is lovely, whatever is commendable, if there is any excellence, if there is anything worthy of praise, think about these things." (Philippians 4:4, 6–8)

Having a family member who is disabled or being disabled yourself, makes daily life difficult, and sometimes frustrating. Responding to unexpected but urgent needs, meeting with doctors or therapists, demands on time and energy, and lack of time to relax emphasize neediness on the part of the caregiver and the one cared for. You may become blind to changes, leading to an absence of joy. If this is your experience, Paul's admonition may seem impossible: rejoicing, not being anxious, thanksgiving, and peace appear out of reach. Thinking about things that are honorable, just, lovely, praiseworthy? Can this include disability?

Earlier, we reflected on God's words to Samuel about not judging by outward appearance (1 Samuel 16:7). Jesus gave similar instructions: "Do not judge by appearances, but judge with right judgment" (John 7:24). This requires looking beyond our circumstances. Focusing only on the limitations and fretting over the problems and needs created by disability engenders a spirit of negativity which keeps us from resting in God's presence. Looking "at," rather than "within" our circumstances, make us lose sight of God's blessings and the peace and hope that he wants for us — and it opens us to Satan's attempts to derail our faith.

Culture has a clear bias toward physical perfection and attractiveness, creating fear of limitation. Disability is seen negatively as "deviance," suggesting that happiness is unavailable to someone with a disability. Paul's words quoted above stress contentment rather than what the world considers happiness. Knowing that God is with us even in the midst of life's struggles or disabling conditions brings encouragement and hope. The Bible shows, through precept and example, that God's sovereignty, wisdom, love, and grace are not threatened by disability, nor is his goodness challenged if he does not intervene to prevent or cure a disabling condition.

Sometimes our attitude is our greatest disability. We need an attitude adjustment, so that instead of seeing *disability* we see *possibility*. Even a severe mental or physical limitation is no obstacle to what God can do, nor does it indicate God's absence or judgment. Disability is not a person's identity. The label "disabled" tells us nothing about who the person is, or may be capable of doing (nor does that label tell us much about what the person *cannot* do). In earlier devotions we have spoken about Sarah (day 5), Sheila (day 7), and Elliot (day 9) and how they, despite being disabled, demonstrate joy and contentment in their lives, and bring blessing to others. Rather than focusing on the disability and the busyness of our day, we need to center on God and his ability. Paul exhorted focusing on things that are worthy of praise. This begins with thinking about God and his goodness. As we contemplate God's love and presence, how we view disability will be changed, and we will begin to see possibilities — ways that we or our disabled loved one can bring joy and blessing to others, and glory to God.

FOR REFLECTION

What attitudes or behaviors do you have that need to be transformed? Read Paul's letter to the Philippian church and reflect on his teaching about joy and contentment in Philippians 4:11-13. How does this teaching apply to your situation?

TAKE ACTION

Begin to see possibilities by intentionally looking for improvements in functioning of the person with the disability. *Expect* growth and keep a record as new abilities emerge. As you become more aware of subtle changes unfolding in your loved one, your attitude will also change from sorrow to joy. Thank God for these changes.

DAY 13

PEACEFUL PARENTING
IN A STORMY LIFE

"May the LORD give strength to his people! May the LORD bless his people with peace!" (Psalm 29:11)

"Let the peace of Christ rule in your hearts, to which indeed you were called in one body. And be thankful." (Colossians 3:15)

Being disabled, or being the parent or spouse of someone with a disability often leaves a person feeling like they are caught in stormy circumstances. Raising a child who is disabled and dealing with negative, prejudicial attitudes of others toward your child (and possibly toward you or your family), may lead to times when you do not feel strong or at peace. Focusing on difficult experiences and being overly concerned about what the future holds for your disabled family member can result in discouragement. It is important to keep your eyes focused on God, drawing strength from him and resting in the peace he gives. Psalm 29 gives assurance that God can strengthen and enable you not only to survive, but to grow through the storms you face. But our focus must be on God, not the storms!

Psalm 29 is a beautiful hymn of praise to God in which David describes a powerful storm moving over the land from the Mediterranean Sea, across Lebanon, and passing into the wilderness. He says the glory of God thunders so powerfully that it splits the cedar trees, makes the mountains tremble, and strips the trees of their leaves. He likens the voice of the Lord to bolts of lightning. But David says that even in these stormy conditions, God sits enthroned over the flood as king forever.

Though David is glorifying God, he is looking outward at the storm. Great storms can be awe-inspiring. There is a fearsome beauty in the storm: thunder roaring, lightning flashing, winds swirling, and rain pelting against the ground. But if caught in such a storm we may experience apprehension and insecurity. Often, the daily responsibility of caring for a family member who is disabled may seem like being caught in a storm of hurricane proportion.

But David did not limit his vision to the storm, and neither should we. Our sight needs to go beyond the storm and settle on God who, as David says, gives strength to his people and blesses them with peace — even in the midst of the tempest. God is still in control as we deal with the "storms" of disability. No storm is so great, no circumstance so distressing, that it can overpower or short-circuit God's love. Life may be hard, but "hard" is not the same as "bad." Living in God's peace does not mean an absence of struggles or problems; the peace that comes from God should rule in our heart and mind (Colossians 3:15). Letting the peace of God rule in your heart impacts how you respond to your daily struggles. Peace in your heart enables praising God with your words.

David described God as sitting enthroned over the flood. To be "over" the flood signifies that God is in control. Because he is a God of love, we are assured that the flood will not completely overwhelm us, but he will give us strength. Take comfort in knowing that God sits enthroned above your struggles as well. Drawing heavily on the peace of God when facing issues related to disability will lead to a state of calm, even though the struggles are not removed. The Christian's lifestyle must be characterized by continual trust in God.

Maintaining this focus will make a difference in your life and witness. God's promises are always truer than your feelings, more affirming than your circumstances.

FOR REFLECTION

God is neither unaware of, nor unconcerned with our struggles. He wants us to live at peace. Spend time reflecting on Isaiah 26:3, John 14:27, and Philippians 4:7.

TAKE ACTION

Make the words of Romans 15:13 your personal prayer: God, my source of hope, fill me with joy and peace because I trust in you. Help me to overflow with confident hope through the power of the Holy Spirit

DAY 14

THE MEASURE OF A MAN OR WOMAN: VALUING WEAKNESS

"But God chose what is foolish in the world to shame the wise; God chose what is weak in the world to shame the strong; God chose what is low and despised in the world, even things that are not, to bring to nothing things that are, so that no human being might boast in the presence of God." (1 Corinthians 1:27-30)

Being or becoming disabled threatens the self-image of people who think themselves fully capable and in control of their lives. But God does not measure people by what they can or cannot do. Nothing we do will make God love us any more than he already does. His love is perfect and unconditional.

God doesn't need our strength, ability, or intelligence. He wants our love and fellowship, our worship and faithfulness — things which don't require having an able body. Abilities and strengths, limitations and disabilities don't define who we are, nor are they a measure of the value of a man, woman, or child. As believers, whether disabled or able-bodied, we belong to God purely by grace. What is important are God's intentions: what God purposes to do through us, even in our weakness, is to display his power.

Paul says God chose what is foolish and weak, low and despised in the world. His words imply mental slowness, feebleness, lack of esteem, and rejection. Many people see folks with disabilities as foolish, weak, or to be despised. But as the parent or spouse of someone with a disability, or being disabled yourself, you know differently. Perhaps you have observed how people who regard themselves as strong are "shamed" when seeing what people with disabilities can accomplish through the strength and gifting of God.

God is pleased to work through people whom cultures disregard, exploit, and even abuse. Many see little value in people with developmental disabilities and have difficulty understanding that God could have a purpose for them. Cordell recognizes this bias, but he has been used by God to accomplish much despite having cerebral palsy. Cordell did not let his physical impairment prevent him from creating a camp and several residential homes for people with disabilities.

Weakness and disability do not mean worthlessness; disability does not mean complete inability. When God looks at someone who has a disability he does not see limited value or possibility; he sees someone through whom he can display his greatness. Paul described us as fragile, easily broken clay pots into which the "light" of the gospel has been placed (2 Corinthians 4:7). But light inside a broken or cracked pot easily shines through the cracks!

Knowing and respecting our weakness helps us become more compassionate and patient, and to experience God's peace. People who are disabled are precious and important. We must value, not fear weakness. We are often unwilling to acknowledge our own brokenness, but quick to find faults in others. As Christians, we are called to be people of peace, not violence (physical or verbal).

God's goal is to show the world that it needs his grace [cf. 2 Corinthians 12:9]. Financial success, fame, worldly status, athletic prowess, etc., do not lead to eternal life. People who trust in these will be put to shame.

FOR REFLECTION

God's truth is often paradoxical, undermining the arguments of those who boast in their wisdom and strength. But Jesus said, "Whoever would be great among you must be your servant" (Matthew 20:26). Where do you find yourself?

TAKE ACTION

In 2 Corinthians 12:7-10 Paul described his struggle with a disabling condition and asked God to remove his "thorn in the flesh." God responded by giving Paul insight into another paradox: God's power is made perfect (complete) as he works in and through our "weakness." Conversely, in our weakness we most clearly experience God's strength. Any "power" we have is ended so that God receives honor in acting through us. Relying on self-effort, blinded by our own strength, can hinder God's activity. What "weakness" in your life is God able to use? Place it in God's hands and watch what he does.

DAY 15

WHERE IS OUR GOD? PSALM 115 GIVES THE ANSWER

"Not to us, O LORD, not to us, but to your name give glory, for the sake of your steadfast love and your faithfulness! Why should the nations say, 'Where is their God?' Our God is in the heavens; he does all that he pleases." (Psalm 115:1-3)

Psalm 115 praises God for his unfailing love and faithfulness and assures us that God is our help and shield. How easily we forget this truth when our focus shifts from God to what is happening in and around us. Life presents many challenges, but as the parent or spouse of someone who is disabled, the challenges become more difficult. These struggles are further amplified when culture, family, friends, or the church wrongly interpret disability as resulting from personal sin, God's punishment, or as proof that God does not exist. Behind these errant ideas is the same question the nations asked of Israel in Psalm 115: "Where is your God?" Their question arose because they did not see any idols of Jehovah being worshiped by the Israelites. Families affected by disability may ask "Where are you, God? Why did you allow disability to enter our lives?" Their question is raised because they cannot "see" God in their situation. Perhaps you have felt this way at times, too.

Does disability call into question the love and sovereignty of God? Why would a "good" God allow this? Dwelling on these questions can lead to self-pity (why me? why my child?), self-doubt (do I not have sufficient faith?), and inappropriate guilt (have I done something to deserve this?). Such spiritual struggles may recur as limitations of the disability become more evident or a disabled child shows delays in reaching developmental milestones.

The answer the psalmist gives is still true today. First, he says "Our God is in the heavens", but this does not mean he is an absentee God who has no concern or is not in sovereign control. Secondly, the psalmist adds that God "does all that he pleases." This does not mean God acts arbitrarily but that whatever God wills or allows is pleasing to him because in the long run, God will be glorified. Disability in itself does not bring pleasure to God any more than warfare does, but disability does not contradict the character of God as all-good and all-loving (1 John 4:8, 16). God remains in control and is actively working things together for his good purposes.

Still, lacking the knowledge and wisdom of God, we may feel that God has abandoned us. What we see as tragic we may attribute to an absence of God's love. But where we see weakness and disability, God sees an opportunity for his grace and power to be displayed. In earlier devotionals we met Sarah, Sheila, Elliot, and Cordell—all individuals with a disability who make themselves available to God, bringing blessing to many and praise to God.

We need to stay mindful of God's loving nature, especially when we face various struggles in life, including those related to disability. God has not promised to prevent or remove these struggles, but he has promised never to leave or forsake us (Hebrews 14:5). Knowing that God walks with us through trials and struggles brings comfort (cf. Psalm 23:4). Focusing on God and his promises helps us to think differently, with renewed minds (Romans 12:2), so that we can praise him in all circumstances. God is pleased when we look to him for strength and allow his power to be displayed in and through our lives and the lives of our disabled loved ones.

FOR REFLECTION

Keep focused on God, who is sovereignly able to bring glory to himself, and on Christ, the incarnation of God's love and our example for living. Reflect on Hebrews 4:15-16, which tells us that Jesus understands and sympathizes with our struggles; he shares in and is affected by what you experience living with disability as part of your family.

TAKE ACTION

Carefully read Psalm 115. List what the psalmist says about God. Find someone you can share this psalm with to bring them comfort and encouragement.

DAY 16

BY THE GRACE OF GOD
I AM WHAT I AM

"By the grace of God I am what I am." (1 Corinthians 15:10)

"For we are his workmanship, created in Christ Jesus for good works, which God prepared beforehand, that we should walk in them." (Ephesians 2:10)

How do we come to terms with our own or a loved one's disability? In the world of disability there are many labels, some coming from the medical or psychological field, others from the cultural arena. These labels are often used to refer to those who are disabled as if the labels capture the essence of the person. But labels, even those that are "officially sanctioned," mask the person by directing attention to the disability. They do not allow discovery of positive attributes of the person, and prevent seeing the blessing the individual with the disability is and can be to others.

The individual with the disability, and all who love and care for that person, must look beyond the limitation to see the *person*. We need to remember that all human beings have been created in the image of God. The image of God is in no way diminished by disability. Ephesians 2:10 declares that we are God's workmanship, created for good works, which God has prepared beforehand for us to do. Even having a severe disability does not limit God's ability to work through the person.

Paul said "by the grace of God I am what I am." He was specifically referring to his appointment by God as an apostle, something which he had not worked to become, though his education and experience as a Pharisee were part of God's preparing him for his true calling. We are not apostles in the same sense as Paul, but Christians are commissioned to proclaim the truth of the gospel to the world (Mark 16:15). Our commissioning, like Paul's, is by the grace of God.

But can a person whose body or mind is "unconventional" because of disability also say "by the grace of God I am what I am" and mean this positively, not just as submissive acceptance of their condition?

Some may ask how allowing a person to be disabled can be an act of grace on the part of God. They focus on how the disability limits the person, but behind their question is fear of disability, and how their life would be different if disabled. The Bible teaches that God has designed every individual and has given at least one spiritual gift to every believer, whether able-bodied or disabled. God expects those gifts and abilities to be used wisely and responsibly in service to him and to others. We must not assume that disability means the person has nothing to offer. Able-bodied persons must not assume that they are better or stronger in ability, knowledge, or spirituality. God's definition of human value and a productive life is vastly different that the world's idea.

Elliot, Sarah, Sheila, and Cordell, whom I have mentioned before, all have a disability, but readily use their *abilities* to lead and to teach others. They would each say, "I am what I am by the grace of God." Care must be taken not to define persons who are disabled by their needs, but to be open to receive the gift which they can be to all of us.

FOR REFLECTION

Jesus, the Son of God, made himself vulnerable by becoming incarnate, just as all humanity is vulnerable. At his crucifixion, he became "paralyzed," unable to move other than to push up with his feet to breathe and move his head from side to side. Is it possible that a person with a disability, by being more openly vulnerable, better "images" God than people who are able-bodied?

Consider how personal weakness or disability may provide opportunity to experience God's presence.

TAKE ACTION

Sometimes we become so used to the limitations shown by a person who is disabled that we overlook signs of growth or change. If we can change the way we look at the person, the way they look will also change.

DAY 17

WHAT ABOUT MY CHILD? CAN SOMEONE WITH A SEVERE DISABILITY BE SAVED?

"And Jesus said to his disciples, 'Truly, I say to you, only with difficulty will a rich person enter the kingdom of heaven. Again I tell you, it is easier for a camel to go through the eye of a needle than for a rich person to enter the kingdom of God.' When the disciples heard this, they were greatly astonished, saying, 'Who then can be saved?' But Jesus looked at them and said, 'With man this is impossible, but with God all things are possible.'" (Matthew 19:23-26)

Some parents of children with severe cognitive or physical disabilities are unsure whether their child is capable of understanding the message of the gospel. It is important to remember that this response is not dependent on our ability, but on God's Spirit working in our heart. It is doubtful that any of us fully understand all that Christ has accomplished through his death on the cross and subsequent resurrection. Salvation is by his grace alone, through faith. Faith is not a matter of intellect; it is a response of love, not understanding, and involves the relationship of our whole self with God.

Still, can a severely mentally or physically challenged child have this faith? The question implies that we must be able to do something, even if only raising our hand or walking down an aisle in response to an evangelist's invitation to "accept" Christ. The answer to the question can be drawn from Jesus' response to his disciples in Matthew 19. After a discussion with a wealthy young man who walked away from Jesus, he told his disciples it is easier for a camel to pass through the eye of a needle than for a wealthy person to enter the kingdom of God. The disciples, assuming wealth is a sign of God's blessing, were astonished and asked "Who then can be saved?" Jesus answered, "With man this is impossible, but with God all things are possible."

This principle relates to individuals who are unable to respond verbally or physically because of disability. What we think doubtful or impossible presents no challenge to God. Knowledge *about* Jesus is not the same as *knowing* Jesus as Lord; head knowledge is not always accompanied by heart knowledge. An adult or a child with a disability may move with difficulty (on not at all) and may be unable to respond verbally, but neither of these limitations should be interpreted as having a soul that cannot be reached by or respond to the Holy Spirit's work. *We* cannot judge who is or is not able to receive the gift of faith. As a Christian parent, your responsibility is to be faithful in making the gospel visible through words and actions, trusting in the broadness of God's grace, which is not restricted by even the most severe disability. People are not saved through any works or reasoning of their own (Ephesians 2:8–10). Even people with profound disabilities can be drawn to Christ through the power of God's grace.

As Christ's representative, we minister to these children out of love, through our actions and words, even though our words may not be understood. "Receiving the gospel" is done with the heart, not the intellect. Ministry depends more on heart-felt obedience and heart-guided actions than on the child's ability to see, hear, walk, talk, or mentally understand our words.

Humanly speaking, salvation may seem hopeless for a severely disabled child, but salvation does not depend on a person's ability, actions, or achievements. With God, however, all things are possible. Salvation is for those who humbly receive God's salvation. Perhaps children with severe disabilities display that humility more than adults.

FOR REFLECTION

Joel 2:32, Acts 2:21, and Romans 10:13 all state that "whoever calls upon the name of the Lord will be saved." Does this necessarily require an audible "call"?

TAKE ACTION

Perhaps you have not thought of your actions and words as sharing the gospel of God's love and grace. Take time to list how you have "been" Christ to your child. Ask God for strength and vision in representing Christ.

DAY 18

WHAT ABOUT MY CHILD? CAN A CHILD WITH A DISABILITY SERVE GOD?

"You were called to freedom, brothers. Only do not use your freedom as an opportunity for the flesh, but through love serve one another." (Galatians 5:13)

"Show hospitality to one another without grumbling. As each has received a gift, use it to serve one another, as good stewards of God's varied grace." (1 Peter 4:9-10)

Paul explained our call to liberty in Christ allows us to freely and lovingly serve others because our focus is not personal benefit. We celebrate our freedom by performing acts of kindness and love designed to advance the welfare of others, fulfilling the law of love (Matthew 22:37-39).

As the parent of a child with a significant disability, your calling involves serving that child, caring for and meeting his or her needs. Peter places service to others in the context of Christian hospitality. Providing protection, physical, emotional, and spiritual support, and promoting growth and development in your child exemplify hospitality. Your actions also embody the gospel for your child. Don't worry about whether your words are understood. Talk and sing about Jesus and pray with your child. Rest in the knowledge that the Lord deeply loves your child.

What about a child who is severely or profoundly disabled? Does the biblical command to serve others apply to that child? Does that child have gifts enabling service to others in a way that brings glory to God?

Severely/profoundly disabled children often more greatly appreciate the love and care they receive than able-bodied children who expect (or demand) to be served. They may be more open to serving others because they are less focused on self and less apt to be tempted by the world.

Following Jesus is about how we live. A relationship with God starts with his call, not with what or how much we know. We cannot assume a severe/profound disability disqualifies a person from being a disciple or that God would not call this person because of a limited understanding of the gospel. "Knowing Jesus" does not require a certain level of intellectual ability; God is not hindered by disability, no matter how severe. Jesus knows the heart of each person (cf. John 2:24-25; Romans 8:27). John the Baptist was filled with the Holy Spirit while still in Elizabeth's womb (Luke 1:15). Having not yet been born, John had no knowledge of Jesus, yet he responded to Jesus' presence, even though Jesus was still in Mary's womb. Following Jesus does not require complete theological understanding of who Jesus is or what he accomplished on the cross. This makes it improper to conclude that someone who is severely or profoundly disabled is unable to "follow" Jesus or to participate in God's healing work in the world. Without speaking a word or performing any action, severely disabled children touch other's lives in powerful ways.

Vanya is a 16 year old boy who is profoundly disabled because of brain damage that occurred at or shortly after birth. He cannot speak, is unable to move voluntarily, and it is not known how much of what he hears is understood. He has been completely dependent on his mother' love and care all his life. Vanya's name means "gracious gift of God," which is exactly how his mother sees him. He extends the gift of God's grace to everyone he meets through his eyes and his smiles, and enjoys the welcome he receives at his church.

This raises a question: the body and mind can be disabled, but can the spirit be disabled? Being able to give and receive love is a distinguishing characteristic of Christianity (cf. John 13:34-35). For Vanya, this quality differentiates him more than his disability.

FOR REFLECTION

Peter said serve others as good stewards of God's varied grace, implying a great diversity in God's gracious gifts. Paul and Peter identified "bigger" spiritual gifts, but their lists are not complete. What examples of God's grace can you identify in your child, despite his or her disability? How does your child minister to you?

TAKE ACTION

Your call as a parent is to live as an obedient servant of Christ, re-presenting Jesus to your child. How can you help your child "see" Jesus?

DAY 19

WHAT ABOUT MY CHILD?
WORSHIPING IN SPIRIT AND TRUTH

"The hour is coming, and is now here, when the true worshipers will worship the Father in spirit and truth, for the Father is seeking such people to worship him. God is spirit, and those who worship him must worship in spirit and truth." (John 4:23-24)

"These I will bring to my holy mountain, and make them joyful in my house of prayer ... for my house shall be called a house of prayer for all peoples." (Isaiah 56:7)

Worship is a time to praise God for who he is and for what he has done through Jesus. Many think the value of worship is in what they "get" out of the service, how inspiring the sermon was. Few seem concerned about what God "gets" out of our worship.

Worship is a time when whole families, adults and children, as part of the collective family of God respond to what God is doing in their hearts and lives. But is a child with physical or cognitive impairments capable of worshiping God? If that child has difficulty sitting still or utters random noises, should he be included in these corporate worship times? Do you feel uncomfortable bringing your child into the worship center, fearing he may disturb others? He may; but, frankly, that is their problem. God will not be disturbed!

Some people define worship in terms of the elements of the Sunday service, much of which a disabled child may not be able to participate in or understand. Should they be present in the Sunday service? What might worship "look like" for such a child?

Children who are non-verbal may be unable to join in much of the worship activity or to express what's going on in their own spirit. However, their body language and facial expression may speak loudly, revealing their response to the Lord. In previous devotional entries, I have spoken about Sarah, Sheila, and Elliot, each of whom is severely disabled but eagerly participates in worship, leading others by their example. Another child who loves the Lord is Ngwe, a young girl we met while serving in Cameroon. Ngwe has cerebral palsy, resulting in awkward movement of her limbs, severe cognitive disability, and an inability to speak. But she's an important part of a children's worship team. When the group sings, Ngwe stands before them, moving her arms as much as she can. We refer to her as the "choir director." Her smile lights up her face as she participates as fully as she is able, leading all who are present at the church into deeper worship of God.

Looking only at Ngwe's outward appearance, some people would regard her as among the "weaker parts of the body" (1 Corinthians 12:12-26). But Paul said the parts of the body that *seem* to be weaker are indispensable. Ngwe, and the other children I have mentioned, may actually be the "stronger ones." They are examples of those who worship God in spirit and truth. We need to remember that God said "My house shall be called a house of prayer for *all* peoples." God does not say only non-disabled are welcome. Psalm 150:6 says, "Let everything that has breath praise the LORD!" Everything that has breath includes *all* living things. If animals can praise God, surely children with disabilities who bear the image of God are able to praise him as well. And perhaps, their praise may be more natural and honest than the worship of non-disabled persons.

FOR REFLECTION

Read Psalm 150 and consider the various methods of praising God. What are ways your child can praise the Lord? Think creatively.

In Luke 18:16-17 Jesus reprimanded the disciples for scolding parents for bringing their young children to Jesus: "Let the children come to me, and do not hinder them, for to such belongs the kingdom of God." Why did Jesus react so strongly? Do Jesus' words apply to children with disabilities?

TAKE ACTION

Consider the different ways people can participate in worship. Does your child respond to the spoken word, to the music, to a visual presentation, to physical participation? Can your child participate by helping to set up the room, serve as a greeter, or be part of a Christmas program?

DAY 20

WHAT ABOUT MY CHILD? CAN GOD USE A CHILD WITH A DISABILITY TO BUILD HIS CHURCH?

"And I tell you, you are Peter, and on this rock I will build my church, and the gates of hell shall not prevail against it." (Matthew 16:18)

"But God chose what is foolish in the world to shame the wise; God chose what is weak in the world to shame the strong; God chose what is low and despised in the world, even things that are not, to bring to nothing things that are, so that no human being might boast in the presence of God." (1 Corinthians 1:27–29)

"Just as I was with Moses, so I will be with you. I will not leave you or forsake you. Be strong and courageous, for you shall cause this people to inherit the land that I swore to their fathers to give them." (Joshua 1:5–6)

The last few devotional studies have considered whether children with severe disabilities can be saved, serve, and worship God. Here, we ask whether God can use a person with a severe disability to build his church. On one level we acknowledge that God is able to do mighty things without the help of human hands. Recall God's response to Sarah's laughter when God said that despite her advanced age, she would have a child: "Is anything too hard [or too wonder-full] for the LORD?" (Genesis 18:14). We know this to be true but when we look at a child with severe disability, especially an intellectual disability, we wonder how he or she can participate in building God's kingdom.

In Matthew 16:18, Jesus said "I will build my church," and he has been doing this through his people ever since. Christ does not always build with strong, healthy, able-bodied believers who possess worldly "status." Rather, Paul declares, Christ builds his church using people seen by the world as weak in order to confound the strong (1 Corinthians 1:27). Peterson's paraphrase is even clearer: "Isn't it obvious that God deliberately chose men and women that the culture overlooks and exploits and abuses, chose these 'nobodies' to expose the hollow pretensions of the 'somebodies'?" (MSG).

Being overlooked, exploited, abused, considered 'nobodies' precisely captures how many in our culture see people with significant disabilities. But God says it is *his* strength that is important. God is not limited by a person's disability; in fact, he accomplishes more through peoples' weakness than through their strength. God equips those he calls for the tasks to which he calls and has designed them, even if that design includes disability. God uses weakness, pain, suffering, or disability to make us aware of our dependence on him.

God instructed Joshua to be strong and courageous, traits the world values but which may be less evident in someone with severe physical or intellectual disability. People are often honored with medals or financially rewarded because of heroism or valor. Some people with disabilities have been viewed as heroes because of outstanding performance despite living with what the world sees as "limitation." It is gratifying to be recognized for accomplishment. But as believers, our intent is to bring glory to God. Strength and courage are drawn from God's presence, being accepted by God despite our disability or weakness, knowing that what we do is done for him.

Mariamu is a young girl from West Africa who was born without arms. This is seen as a tragedy in the shame-based culture of her family which leads them to surmise that her life has no value. Those who don't take time to get to know her question her ability to serve God. But Mariamu knows Jesus as her Lord and Savior, and joyfully —boldly and courageously — participates in praise and worship, raising her legs and clapping with her feet in community with others who echo her motions with their arms and hands. And Mariamu uses her abilities to serve others in the center where she lives who have more severe limitations, even gently feeding them holding a spoon with her toes. Mariamu exemplifies the spirit commanded in Joshua 1:5–6; she knows that God is present with her wherever she goes. Mariamu models a life lived in loving submission to the Lord. She is an example for us to follow.

FOR REFLECTION

How do you view your child or other loved one who has a disability? In the midst of caring for them and seeking to meet their physical and emotional needs, it is easy to overlook their strength and character. In what ways do they reveal to you their strength even though disabled? How do you convey to them (and to others) that they are valued and valuable?

God promised that he would always be with Joshua, but Joshua required reminders to be strong and courageous (Joshua 1:6, 7, 9, 18) as did his men (10:25). It is easy to feel overwhelmed and weak in the busyness of life, especially when someone has a disability. What can you do to keep your focus on God's promise to be with you and his command to be strong?

DAY 21

GREAT EXPECTATIONS: WHAT GOD CAN TEACH ME THROUGH MY CHILD

"Behold, children are a heritage from the LORD, the fruit of the womb a reward." (Psalm 127:3)

"A glad heart makes a cheerful face, but by sorrow of heart the spirit is crushed. ... All the days of the afflicted are evil, but the cheerful of heart has a continual feast." (Proverbs 15:13, 15)

"Weeping may tarry for the night, but joy comes with the morning." (Psalm 30:5b)

Yesterday's devotional considered how a child with a severe disability can bring glory to God through serving others. Here we consider what God is able to teach us through that child.

You may wonder how the verses quoted above fit together. Giving birth to a child with a disability or having a child who became disabled through illness or injury raises practical and spiritual questions. At first, you proudly claimed Psalm 127:3 and thanked God for his blessing. But you experienced a change in mood from gladness of heart and a cheerful face to a sorrowful heart and a crushed spirit when your child's disability was identified and you realized the lifelong implications of disability for your child, yourself, and your marriage. This is not where you envisioned yourself being as a mom or dad. The great expectations you had when anticipating the birth of this child have likely disappeared. But perhaps all that is needed is a change in focus.

Being open to what God wants us to learn from a child with a severe disability requires eyes that see the child's beauty beneath the limitations and hearts that remain accessible to God and his promise never to leave or forsake us (Hebrews 13:5). As we remain open to God's Spirit, and approach our children with thanksgiving and love, there is much God can teach us, including unconditional love, acceptance, patience, tolerance, perseverance, and dependence on God. We recognize our own vulnerability and become more ready to show forgiveness. We learn how much we need the Holy Spirit to develop fruit in our lives (Galatians 5:22-23). This helps us become more skilled in lovingly serving others.

This is not to suggest that God intentionally disabled your child in order to present you with an object lesson. But Romans 11:36 says all things—including your disabled child — are from and through and to God, and designed to bring him glory and honor. Day 14's devotional considered God's deliberate choice of the "weak" to confound people who think themselves strong, to prevent them from boasting before God and to show the need for God's grace. Yesterday's devotional dealt with how a disabled child can serve God. It is important to remember God is working in you and in your disabled child in ways that we often do not fully grasp. He wants us to rest in his sovereign love, maintain an eternal perspective, and know that though there are times of weeping, joy comes in the morning. Sadness or depression can make it difficult to get through the day without stress, but with God, life can become like a continuous feast even in the midst of adversity.

The key is not to keep your lost dreams or present circumstances as your point of focus. Instead, keep your eyes fixed on Jesus (Hebrews

12:2). Your expectations of and for you child may need adjustment, but Jesus never changes. As Isaiah wrote, God will keep in perfect peace those who steadfastly keep their mind on him (Isaiah 26:3).

FOR REFLECTION

Romans 8:28 speaks of God's ability to bring good out what we may perceive as a bad situation. How does this apply to our understanding of how disability and God's sovereignty relate? What is needed for you to remain focused on the "good" that God has and can continue to bring through your child?

Proverbs 3:5-8 instructs us to trust in the Lord not our own understanding, and to acknowledge him. As you put this into practice, God will bring healing and refreshment to your spirit.

TAKE ACTION

Start keeping a record of things God teaches you through your child. Thank God for his blessings.

DAY 22

WHAT WE WILL BE HAS NOT YET APPEARED: LIVING BETWEEN TWO WORLDS

"But he said to me, 'My grace is sufficient for you, for my power is made perfect in weakness.' Therefore I will boast all the more gladly of my weaknesses, so that the power of Christ may rest upon me. For the sake of Christ, then, I am content with weaknesses, insults, hardships, persecutions, and calamities. For when I am weak, then I am strong." (2 Corinthians 12:9-10)

"Beloved, we are God's children now, and what we will be has not yet appeared; but we know that when he appears we shall be like him, because we shall see him as he is." (1 John 3:2)

The Bible teaches that every human being is created in the image of God. The image of God is something we *are,* not an attribute we possess, such as the ability to reason, creativity, communication, or relationality. These attributes are merely consequences of being in God's image. The most severely or profoundly physically or cognitively limited individual is no less God's image than the intellectual genius who lives down the street. God honors all people; they are equally his by creation and are equally loved.

In 2 Corinthians 12, Paul related his struggle with a disabling condition and how he pleaded with God to remove his "thorn in the flesh." In response to Paul's anguished prayers, God explained that it is in our weakness and limitations that we most clearly experience

God's strength. God's power is made perfect (complete) in our weakness. Any "power" we have in ourselves comes to an end so that God alone receives honor by acting through us. Relying on self-effort, as if blinded by our own strength, may hinder God's activity.

When God looks at someone who is disabled, he does not see limited value or possibility; he sees someone through whom he can display his greatness. What do you see? Paul reminds us that we are what we are by God's grace. Being disabled, or having a loved one who is disabled, does not mean God's grace is absent. In an earlier devotional, we saw from 1 Corinthians 1:27-30 that God uses what the world considers weak, foolish, or despised so that people cannot boast in his presence. We also considered Jesus' words in John 9 about the man's blindness providing opportunity for the works of God to be displayed in him. That work of God was the man's coming to faith. The cure of his blindness was a bonus; his salvation was not dependent on the cure.

Understanding God's response transformed Paul's view of his "thorn." Rather than considering it a messenger of Satan meant to weaken him, he accepted his "thorn" as a gift, a blessing from God. Rather than removing it, God gave Paul grace *in his "handicap,"* saying that through Paul's weakness God's strength can be more fully displayed. Paul became free to "boast" in his weakness, allowing God to receive the glory.

From a Christian standpoint, therefore, disability is not necessarily something to be gotten rid of. It can actually be a tool or a vessel for God to bring blessing to people and glory to himself, as a testimony to his grace and provision.

Paul and John agree that what we are presently — able-bodied or disabled — does not compare to what we shall be. As believers, we live between the times: between the present, earthly world, where disability and limitations are common, and the future, heavenly, world where we shall be like Jesus. But even as we anticipate that future day, we are being transformed into the image of Christ, even in our disability. Change is coming!

FOR REFLECTION

"My grace is sufficient for you, for my power is made perfect in weakness" (2 Corinthians 12:9). As you contemplate these words of Paul, how do they affect your view of disability and weakness? Can you see in your disabled loved one how God values weakness more than personal strength?

TAKE ACTION

Consider how this perspective on power and weakness differs from the world's perspective. What weaknesses, limitations, or problems in your life is God able to use? How are you encouraged by this passage when you consider disability's impact on your family?

DAY 23

CAN JOY BE FOUND IN THE MIDST OF DISABILITY?

"Count it all joy, my brothers, when you meet trials of various kinds, for you know that the testing of your faith produces steadfastness. And let steadfastness have its full effect, that you may be perfect and complete, lacking in nothing ... Blessed is the man who remains steadfast under trial, for when he has stood the test he will receive the crown of life, which God has promised to those who love him." (James 1:2-4, 12)

"May the God of hope fill you with all joy and peace in believing, so that by the power of the Holy Spirit you may abound in hope." (Romans 15:13)

Any concordance will show that the Bible says a great deal about joy. But when disability is part of your experience, joy can seem elusive. Disability is not sought after, and generally leads to an acute sense of loss. If you or a loved one is disabled, you may cycle repeatedly through periods of grief. Can joy leading to hope be found in the midst of these trials?

James says "count it all joy" when encountering various trials arising from external circumstances, because they serve a purpose. Trials are "testings" meant to prove our faith — more precisely, to *improve* or strengthen our faith. They serve to make us more secure in our faith as we look to God in trust, instead of being overwhelmed by our circumstances. Paul knew this and prayed "May you be strengthened with all power, according to God's glorious might, for all endurance and patience *with joy*" (Colossians 1:11). Joy is not "happiness," which depends on circumstances. Biblical joy "depends" on the Lord. It is an inner quality, a deep assurance or calm delight, drawn from faith in God. It rests on God's loving, gracious, and all-knowing nature, and trusting him. God does not make mistakes. If he allows or brings disability into our life, it is with a righteous purpose.

Outlook determines outcomes; attitude determines action. We have a choice: to focus on our circumstances or on God *despite* our circumstances. The first option leads to negative outcomes — dismay, depression, or anger (directed at the "oppression" or toward God). The second option leads to positive actions — joy in the Lord, holiness of character, deepened faith, and a closer relationship with God.

James speaks about steadfastness, an active intention to endure which results in strength to move forward. Rather than working against us, testing is beneficial. Paul wrote that for those who love God and are called according to his purposes, all things work together for good (Romans 8:28).

Romans 15:13 reminds us that God is a God of hope from whom comes joy and peace in believing. Hope brings tranquility and rest, the opposite of chaos and disorder. God's desire is that hope and joy overflow in our lives.

When I met Tanya, she was 4 ½ years old, physically — a beautiful child, with a bright smile. Developmentally, however, she was much younger. When Tanya was a little more than 2 years old, no one noticed as she wandered from the family gathering on her grandparents' farm. When they searched for her, she was found lying in a stream, face down. They were able to revive her, but it quickly became obvious that she had experienced brain damage from lack of oxygen. Yet her mother was not without hope. She explained that

Tanya had been "born again" and needed to relearn movement and language skills. When I worked with Tanya, she had regained the ability to walk, but was being fitted with leg braces to help her feet and ankles work more efficiently, allowing more fluid movement. And Tanya was beginning to use expressive language again (the word she used most often was "no," always accompanied with a big smile as if she was proud to able to say the word).

Tanya's mom was encouraged, first because God had preserved Tanya's life, and second because Tanya was slowly regaining skills. It was too soon to know if Tanya would have additional cognitive limitations because of the damage to her brain, but her mom remained positive and hopeful. The words of the psalmist capture her outlook: "You have put more joy in my heart than they have when their grain and wine abound. In peace I will both lie down and sleep; for you alone, O LORD, make me [and my daughter] dwell in safety" (Psalm 4:7-8).

FOR REFLECTION

James 1:2 speaks of "various kinds" of trials or testings. The word used can mean *many-colored*. Does thinking of your "testings" as being varicolored, like a beautiful flower garden, change your outlook? Does this lighten the load?

TAKE ACTION

How can you "grow" joy in your life? A primary source of joy is meditation on God's Word. But is also comes from fellowshipping with caring believers, remaining positive, and remembering God's promises. Keep a record of God's goodness in your life and the life of your disabled loved one. Celebrate what God has done.

DAY 24

CAN YOU SEE JESUS?
CAN YOU BE JESUS?

"Whoever receives one such child in my name receives me." (Matthew 18:5)

"Then the King will say to those on his right, 'Come, you who are blessed by my Father, inherit the kingdom prepared for you from the foundation of the world. For I was hungry and you gave me food, I was thirsty and you gave me drink, I was a stranger and you welcomed me, I was naked and you clothed me, I was sick and you visited me, I was in prison and you came to me.' ... And the King will answer them, 'Truly, I say to you, as you did it to one of the least of these my brothers, you did it to me.'" (Matthew 25:34-36, 40)

Raising a child or caring for a spouse who is disabled, meeting their physical, emotional, and spiritual needs, places great demands on your time and energy. Sometimes you may become frustrated, like the umpteenth time you taught them how to do something by themselves. This reaction reveals a momentary lapse in understanding the sacredness of your ministry. "Seeing" Jesus in the individual helps clarify your vision and relieve the sense of burden.

In Matthew 18, Jesus said receiving a little child in his name is to welcome *him*. In Matthew 25, he said ministry done to those in need is ministry done to him. We envision Jesus sitting on a heavenly throne, but this teaching suggests otherwise, at least figuratively. Jesus can be found today in unimagined places and unanticipated people.

We often fail to "see" Jesus either because we aren't looking for him or we don't expect to "see" him, certainly not in persons with significant limitations of disability. But in the parable of the sheep and goats (Matthew 25) Jesus identifies with people in need, saying "I" was hungry, thirsty, a stranger, naked, sick, imprisoned. Jesus sees ministering to people with needs as being done to him. We do no harm to Jesus' teaching by adding physically or mentally disabled to those with whom he identifies. Jesus says that such ministry should be a routine part of our activity — not to receive Christ's blessing, but because of the grace we have already received. Faithfulness is demonstrated by our actions. Showing love and compassion to needy individuals, such as those with disabilities (in our family and in the community) honors God because they, like us, are people of worth and bear the image and likeness of God.

If our spiritual eyes are open, we see in those we care for something of Jesus. At the same time, we "become" Jesus to them, sharing his compassion. Jesus not only did something *for us* on the cross, he has done something *in us,* making us participants in the story of God's love. As the body of Christ, we are to be his loving presence in the world today, to be his hands and voice bringing — more importantly, *being* — he gospel message. We model Jesus' love when we perform acts of kindness such as those described in Matthew 25 as if ministering directly to Jesus, without expectation of reward from the recipients of our ministry.

The individuals I've mentioned in these devotionals are people through whom the glory and brightness of Jesus shines despite — or in some cases, because of — their disability. Keep your eyes open to "see" Jesus in those you care for, and "be" Jesus to them in your actions and attitude. God may want you to learn something about him (or yourself) as you minister in Jesus' name. Ask yourself, "How have I experienced God's grace in ministering to _____? How have I shown God's grace to _____?'

FOR REFLECTION

"Receive" in Matthew 18:5 means to intentionally welcome someone, spiritually and physically, seeing that person as Jesus while being Jesus to the person. How does this apply to your care and support of your disabled loved one?

TAKE ACTION

How can you cultivate a capacity for seeing signs of God's grace, and for being a sign of God's grace as you care for your disabled loved one? How can you become more Christlike in the midst of your activity?

DAY 25

FINDING AND GIVING COMFORT

"Blessed be the God and Father of our Lord Jesus Christ, the Father of mercies and God of all comfort, who comforts us in all our affliction, so that we may be able to comfort those who are in any affliction, with the comfort with which we ourselves are comforted by God ... Indeed, we felt that we had received the sentence of death. But that was to make us rely not on ourselves but on God who raises the dead." (2 Corinthians 1:3-4)

People like to believe they are immune to significant problems. Even Christians may wrongly believe God will not allow them to encounter major difficulties. A study of the life of the Apostle Paul, however, suggests otherwise. Being a Christian does not prevent you, or someone in your family, from becoming disabled. God never promised to prevent or remove things we don't want, but he has promised never to leave or forsake us (Joshua 1:5, Hebrews 12:5).

When disability interrupts your life, it usually comes suddenly, whether in being told your new baby has cerebral palsy, or as the result of an accident or serious illness. The challenges faced are many: Theologically, you question God ("Why?") or try to bargain with God, making promises which cannot be kept. Practically, you imagine a worst case scenario of how life for you or your disabled loved one will be impacted. Emotionally, you wonder how your friends and extended family will react: will they be supportive, turn away, or judge. Your reaction reveals your understanding of God and of disability. Your emotions are stretched, your anxiety high. What brings you comfort in this situation?

Psalm 121:1-2 asks "From where does my help come?" and answers "My help comes from the Lord who made heaven and earth." The word "help" refers to both material and spiritual aid or support; in short, comforting. In 2 Corinthians, Paul praises God as the Father of mercies or compassion, and the God of all comfort who comforts us in our afflictions. Some translations describe God as the *source* of compassion; others make compassion an adjective and describe God as *compassionate Father*. I suggest we think of God as the *definition* of compassion since, as John says, love is the very essence of God (1 John 4:8, 16).

Paul's teaching is not new. David said God is near to the brokenhearted (Psalm 34:18). Isaiah spoke of God's bringing comfort and compassion to his people (Isaiah 49:13, 66:13). God's nature and character are consistent and do not depend on your life circumstances (Malachi 3:6, James, 1:17, Hebrews 13:8). Paul suffered in many ways but was comforted by God, which enabled him to comfort others. Living a victorious Christian life does not require the absence of disability, only that our heart be right with God.

The answer to the question "Where do I find compassion or comfort?" is: from God, the Father of compassion. Knowing that God is with us *always* brings comfort, especially when others turn away. But we are not to hoard God's compassion. We are to be a conduit for his love and compassion to flow to others. Coming alongside others actualizes God's love as you "enact" comfort to them in the midst of their struggles. Spiritual development ensues as we respond properly to trials, and is demonstrated in an increased recognition of God's ongoing love and presence, a deepened dependence upon God, and an increased thankfulness even in the midst of suffering or trials. Jesus' ultimate purpose is to bring God's people into rest (Matthew 11:28-30). As he compassionately comforts you, share that compassion with others.

FOR REFLECTION

Read 1 Corinthians 1:3-11 and consider God's purposes in your sometimes painful experiences. Jot down your thoughts in answer to these questions: Difficult times help me to know God as _____ (1:3). Difficult times prepare me to _____ (1:4-7). Difficult times teach me to _____ (1:8-9). Difficult times give me _____ (1:10).

TAKE ACTION

Who do you know that needs the comfort you and your disabled loved one can bring to them? Perhaps someone just beginning their journey with disability or someone in your church who is struggling with life?

DAY 26

GOD IS YOUR ABBA

"For all who are led by the Spirit of God are sons of God. For you did not receive the spirit of slavery to fall back into fear, but you have received the Spirit of adoption as sons, by whom we cry, 'Abba! Father!' The Spirit himself bears witness with our spirit that we are children of God, and if children, then heirs—heirs of God and fellow heirs with Christ" (Romans 8:14-16a)

"For we do not have a high priest who is unable to sympathize with our weaknesses, but one who in every respect has been tempted as we are, yet without sin. Let us then with confidence draw near to the throne of grace, that we may receive mercy and find grace to help in time of need." (Hebrews 4:15-16)

We all have fathers: some good, others not so good; some tyrannical, some absent. We all have ideas of what a father should be like. When I was a child, "Father Knows Best" was a popular television program. I don't recall if he *really* knew best, but in those days, being a father meant more than just a physical relationship. My Dad worked 60+ hours each week to provide for our family's needs and Mom did most of the parenting.

As with families not affected by disability, when there is a child with severe impairments, it is usually Mom who is the primary caregiver and Dad is the breadwinner. Nevertheless, it is important for Dad to be included as much as possible lest he feels pushed to the sidelines. Fathers may not always know best, but they are important. Our heavenly Father is even more important.

Whatever your experience with "fathers" has been, what a joy it is to know God as our Father and we are his children. Paul wrote to the Christians in Rome that we have been adopted into God's family. God is our "Abba," a term of endearment akin to "Daddy" or "Papa." Abba signifies a childlike, trusting relationship with God. To formally address our parents as "Mother" or "Father" distances us from them. "Mommy" and "daddy" are more intimate terms that acknowledge our dependence while assuming mutuality of love. Most often Jesus called God "Father" (pater). But when praying in the Garden of Gethsemane he used the double address — "Abba, Father" — revealing both the intensity of his emotions in anticipation of his arrest and crucifixion, and the depth of his relationship with God. In the same way, for us to cry "Abba, Father" implies God's Lordship and our dependency and, knowing the character of God, it also draws on his love and grace.

When you were a young child, you probably called for Daddy when something was not going well or when you wanted to share your joy with him. The thought that your Daddy would not be interested probably never entered your mind as you poured your heart out to him. This is the kind of relationship we have with God. Our Abba wants us to share with him our pains, sorrows, needs, and joys. He cares more deeply for us than our earthly fathers.

Paul says it is through the Holy Spirit that we "cry, 'Abba! Father!" What a privilege we have as children of God! The word "cry" expresses the deep emotion, the urgency of our prayer. It suggests not simply weeping, but screaming — audibly or in our heart —because of frustration, exhaustion, or need. Yet we do this confidently, as God's children, knowing he wants us to come to him and he is ready to respond.

FOR REFLECTION

Hebrews 4:15-16 tells us that Christ understands and is touched by our experiences. He is not offended when we pour out our "bothers" to him in prayer. Who better to turn to when discouragement, stress, or fatigue sets in? How does the author say he responds? How does your awareness of the understanding nature of Christ help in your struggles with disability?

TAKE ACTION

How does thinking of God as "Daddy" encourage you? How have you experienced this relationship in your journey in the world of disability? What other benefits of this relationship have you experienced?

DAY 27

UNFAILING HOPE

"'The LORD your God is in your midst, a mighty one who will save; he will rejoice over you with gladness; he will quiet you by his love; he will exult over you with loud singing. I will gather those of you who mourn for the festival, so that you will no longer suffer reproach. Behold, at that time I will deal with all your oppressors. And I will save the lame and gather the outcast, and I will change their shame into praise and renown in all the earth. At that time I will bring you in, at the time when I gather you together; for I will make you renowned and praised among all the peoples of the earth, when I restore your fortunes before your eyes,' says the LORD." (Zephaniah 3:17-20)

John 5 tells of a man who has been disabled for 38 years and seems to have no hope. When Jesus asked "Do you want to be cured?" he responded "I have no one to help me." Perhaps there have been times when you feel this loneliness and hopelessness.

Zephaniah's words need to be in your heart and mind when facing issues of disability. They bring assurance by pointing to the faithfulness of God, to his love and rejoicing over people (including the disabled), and to his promise to convert shame into praise.

Notice what Zephaniah describes God doing for his people: saving, rejoicing, quieting, exulting, and singing. As you struggle with issues surrounding disability, you may wonder if God still engages in these activities.

If you are disquieted, not rejoicing or singing triumphantly, you may fear that God is displeased or has left you to your own limited resources. But the words are God's; he is telling us he is present, rejoicing, and singing over his people. Disability does not hide us from God, nor does God hide himself because his people are disabled.

Paul called God a God of hope and asked him to fill the Christians with joy and peace so they may abound in hope by the power of the Holy Spirit (Romans 15:13). Hope implies waiting; hope *from God* implies assurance.

The gospel message brings hope, not simply for eternal life, but life and hope with present implications, especially amidst struggles. Knowing God is with us gives hope in the face of affliction and uncertainty so that we can move forward confidently. The Bible affirms that God's sovereignty, wisdom, love, and grace are not threatened by disability. We may grieve what is lost by becoming disabled or what may never be (if born with a significant disability), but God remains our source of hope. Release your expectations and adjust to a "new normal" in the strength that he gives and in the hope that he is.

Remember Jeremiah's words: "The steadfast love of the LORD never ceases; his mercies never come to an end; they are new every morning; great is your faithfulness. 'The LORD is my portion,' says my soul, 'therefore I will hope in him'" (Lamentations 3:22–24).

Be assured: "The LORD is good, a stronghold in the day of trouble; he knows those who take refuge in him" (Nahum 1:7). Disability is not stronger than God, nor can it prevent a person from knowing and serving God.

Zephaniah 3:17 says God "will quiet you in his love." The Hebrew words carry the image of resting, or "pillowing" in God's love, much like parents cradling a child in their arms, surrounding the child with their love. What better place to be when life seems difficult!

FOR REFLECTION

Meditate on Zephaniah 3:17 and the idea of God rejoicing over you with gladness. An alternate reading of the verse says God will calm you with his love. How can you maintain this hopeful focus?

TAKE ACTION

There is stress in dealing with disability, but the degree of stress may fluctuate over time. Satan will prompt doubts about God's faithfulness, causing difficulty resting in the Lord and causing you to withdraw into aloneness. Waiting on the Lord is more doable in the company of other believers. Who can you turn to when you need encouragement?

DAY 28

HAPPINESS OR HOLINESS: WHICH IS PREFERRED?

"Do not be conformed to this world, but be transformed by the renewal of your mind, that by testing you may discern what is the will of God, what is good and acceptable and perfect." (Romans 12:2)

"Rejoice always, pray without ceasing, give thanks in all circumstances; for this is the will of God in Christ Jesus for you." (1 Thessalonians 5:16-18)

How much time and emotional energy have you spent wishing the past had been different or worrying about the future? Such mental scheming is so common it seems to be the way of the world. But this allows the world to control your mind and squeeze you into its mold.

When disability strikes a family, the ensuing grief provides fertile ground for this thinking. Cultural attitudes powerfully affect how people view those who are differently-abled. Even the word "disability" connotes negativity and uncertainty regarding outcomes. Some people incorrectly associate disability with sin, punishment, and lack of faith. You may fall into this pattern of thinking, searching for a reason or purpose for your loved one's disability.

Yielding yourself to God's will is fundamental to living a God-honoring life. This allows trusting that God's will and his actions are linked to his righteousness and love. Paul's exhortation not to be conformed to cultural patterns applies to worldly thinking about disability and God. Being transformed through renewal of your mind allows knowing experientially God's purposes in your life and enables you to dismiss the world's idea of "happiness" and live peacefully with disability. Slowness of physical or cognitive development of a disabled child or the limitations resulting from an acquired impairment will not change. What changes is the way you think, allowing acceptance of disability as a part of your family's life. Don't waste energy fighting, denying, or hiding disability; this can negatively impact your spiritual development. Transformation does not happen overnight; it is an ongoing process as you continually offer yourself to God and are molded more and more into the image of Christ. This "metamorphosis" requires fixing your attention on God, not your circumstances, and not listening to worldly ideas regarding disability.

Your thinking and behavior must be entirely renovated; refusing the norms of conduct and thought employed by the world whenever they are not in accord with God's revealed will and prescribed patterns of behavior. Do not listen to the world's mistaken ideas about disability; listen to God's Word. This demands prayer and surrender of your whole self — body, mind, and will — trusting God to lead and protect [cf. Psalm 23:4]. This, says Paul, will lead to growth in the knowledge of God and to walking "his way," thereby verifying that God's will is good and perfect.

Paul said to rejoice always, pray without ceasing, and give thanks in all circumstances, for this is God's will in Christ Jesus for us (1 Thessalonians 5:16-18). Rejoicing, praying, and giving thanks *in all things* appears to be a tall order when dealing with disability and the daily responsibilities that ensue. But Paul does not say *disability* is the will of God. Rejoicing, praying, and giving thanks in all situations, however, is God's desire for us.

Culturally derived thinking can be a downer, emotionally and spiritually. But, if you are down on your knees in prayer and thanksgiving, acknowledging your dependence on God and trusting that his will is best — that is a good place to be. Holiness of living is better that what the world calls "happiness."

FOR REFLECTION

Meditate of the familiar Psalm 23, noting what David say God does as his Shepherd. Note particularly verse 4 which speaks of God's being with him even in the difficult times. Store the words of promised comfort in your heart.

TAKE ACTION

Paul gives instructions in Romans 12:10-18: cling to what is good; honor one another; be joyful in hope, patient in affliction, faithful in prayer; rejoice with those who rejoice, mourn with those who mourn; live in harmony, do not be proud, be willing to associate with people of low position; be careful to do what is right; live at peace with everyone. Make this a daily commitment. Keep a log of your thoughts and actions. Ask God to give you a pure heart.

DAY 29

WEEPING TO JOY, MOURNING TO DANCING

"Weeping may tarry for the night, but joy comes with the morning ... You have turned for me my mourning into dancing; you have loosed my sackcloth and clothed me with gladness, that my glory may sing your praise and not be silent. O LORD my God, I will give thanks to you forever!" (Psalm 30:5b, 11-12)

"Just as I was with Moses, so I will be with you. I will not leave you or forsake you." (Joshua 1:5)

Imagine the following scenario. You spent months waiting for your child to be born. Throughout the pregnancy countless hours were consumed imagining the new baby and the joy he or she would bring into your life. But in the delivery room you noticed unusual activity among the medical staff who huddled around your newborn. After what seemed an eternity, they told you your new baby has a disability. This unexpected news brought confusion to your mind and grief to your heart. You began to mourn the "death" of the healthy child you had dreamt about. Instantly, your family's identity changed from "normal" to a family affected by disability.

In times like this many parents feel lost and abandoned by God. They begin to question God's wisdom and love, or suspect they have or have not done something that contributed to the child being disabled. Though you plead with God to "fix" the child, in God's love and omniscience, he sees nothing to be fixed. He sees a child who bears his image.

If this has not been your experience, praise the Lord! For many, the journey raising a disabled child may bring repeated battles with fear, anger, and uncertainty. But there will also be repeated times of joy, hope, and peace as you learn to trust God more deeply.

You quickly realize there is a new "normal" in your journey as a family. Learning will be ongoing as you tackle challenges parenting a child who is disabled. Responding to medical and developmental issues your child faces may necessitate periodic reinventing of family roles. Every family undergoes refashioning as roles and expectations change, but having a disabled child, these challenges can be more stressful. Your world is different from that of almost everyone you know. Friends and family may, out of ignorance or fear, sever relationships with you and your child. You begin to feel isolated and alone.

A "new normal" involves accepting that issues faced raising a child with a disability, or faced by the child himself, are beyond your control, but can be surmounted with God's help. This changed perspective is as much a gift from God as is your child. The secret is found in God's promise of continued presence, and releasing your tension and anxiety to God. Constant fretting over these times of difficulty is a form of selfishness because your eyes are not on the Lord but on your circumstances. But the difficult times are only temporary. The words of the psalmist can be your own as your heart remains focused on God: weeping and mourning are temporary; they will be replaced by joy, dancing, and gladness. Sing your praise, do not be silent, and give thanks to the Lord. You are not alone; God has not forsaken you or your family (Joshua 1:5).

Joy comes in "the morning." As you surrender your will to God, embrace his love, and embrace your child, including his disability, God will turn mourning into dancing. Rely on God, not yourself. Admonish yourself with the words of the psalmist: "Why are you cast down, O my soul, and why are you in turmoil within me? Hope in God; for I shall again praise him, my salvation" (Psalm 42:5).

FOR REFLECTION

What new insights do you gain from Psalm 30 about God and his character? How successful have your attempts to change your mourning into dancing in your own strength and determination been?

TAKE ACTION

In what ways do you need God to turn your mourning into dancing? With whom can you share the insights gained from Psalm 30?

DAY 30

COPING WITH DAILY DEMANDS OF DISABILITY

"Then he said to them, 'Go your way. Eat the fat and drink sweet wine and send portions to anyone who has nothing ready, for this day is holy to our Lord. And do not be grieved, for the joy of the LORD is your strength.'" (Nehemiah 8:10)

"Blessed is he whose help is the God of Jacob, whose hope is in the LORD his God, who made the heaven and the earth, the sea, and all that is in them, who keeps faith forever." (Psalm 146:5-6)

"May the God of hope fill you with all joy and peace in believing, so that by the power of the Holy Spirit you may abound in hope." (Romans 15:13)

For a family dealing with disability, peace may seem a rare commodity. Daily struggles in assisting a family member who is disabled, coupled with the usual daily chores can be a heavy load. This, combined with trying to balance work and home life, often leads to a loss of peace. Joy and hope may also seem in short supply. Unable to dredge up energy to meet life's demands on your own, you readily acknowledge the need for the strength which God is, and provides through the Holy Spirit.

Isaiah wrote that God keeps in perfect peace those whose mind is stayed on him, who trust him (Isaiah 26:3). This peace is different from peace offered by the world. Biblical peace (shalom) is a state of completeness and well-being arising from an awareness of God's presence. There is never a time when God removes his presence from us; his Holy Spirit lives within each believer. Knowing his continuing presence should lead to patience, but going through stretches of time when God's presence is not felt can cause your patience to dwindle. In the busyness of life and all that caring for a person who is disabled involves, you may easily become impatient — with yourself, with your situation, with others, and even with God.

We know God is with us in the "good" times, but what about when we are struggling just to get through another day? The Bible clearly teaches that he is also with us in the midst of busyness, sorrows, doubts, and anxieties. These are times when we must be more intentional about being patient, in order to discern the subtle reminders of his love. Perspective matters; when we feel we need God more than ever, he may actually be closer than we realize. His desire is to lead us to grow in our faith.

In Nehemiah 8, following the reading of God's law, the people wept because of awareness of their sin. Nehemiah encouraged them by asserting that this was a day of celebration. He told them, "go your way; do not be grieved, for the joy of the Lord is your strength." We can apply this same principle to ourselves when we feel overwhelmed by the responsibility created by disability in the family. When we are vulnerable to despair, we need assurance that God is present and we need the rest that accompanies knowing that the joy of the Lord is our strength. Joy comes from taking God at his word and acting in faith; it is much more than a "good feeling" based on positive circumstances. Coping with disability and the issues it brings is made possible when we recognize, as did David, that God is for us "a hiding place," that he will guard us in our distress or troubles, that he will encircle us with shouts of joy and deliverance (Psalm 32:7). The joy of the Lord is your strength!

FOR REFLECTION

Reflect on Romans 15:13. Turn the words of Pauls' benediction into a daily prayer to be filled with joy and peace, and to overflow with hope by the power of the Holy Spirit.

TAKE ACTION

How can each day be a day of celebration despite the impact of disability on your family? Perhaps the family can share something which happened or something they learned that is worth celebrating, no matter how small or insignificant it seems. Recognizing and recording the "positives" of each day, the signs of God's continued presence, will help you understand that the joy of the Lord is your strength.

DAY 31

SLOW DOWN AND APPRECIATE
THE MOMENT

*"Trust in the LORD, and do good; dwell in the land and
befriend faithfulness. Delight yourself in the LORD,
and he will give you the desires of your heart. Commit
your way to the LORD; trust in him, and he will act.
He will bring forth your righteousness as the light, and
your justice as the noonday. Be still before the LORD
and wait patiently for him; fret not yourself over the one
who prospers in his way, over the man who carries out
evil devices! ... But the meek shall inherit the land and
delight themselves in abundant peace." (Psalm 37:3-7, 11)*

"Be still, and know that I am God." (Psalm 46:10a)

Everyone leads a busy and somewhat stressful life. But for a family
affected by disability, especially in a child, while some days may
be easier, stress is generally higher than in families not dealing with
disability.

Jordy was born with cerebral palsy. As long as he remained in
a flexed position, his muscles were at ease, but even the slightest
movement caused a spastic reaction in the muscles of his legs, arms,
neck, and torso, leaving him in a stiff, extended position from which
he could not recover. Jordy's parents had to learn new parenting skills,
including how to handle, position, and feed him properly. There
were frequent visits to medical specialists, often at a distance from
his home, and regular appointments with physical and occupational
therapists. Early intervention services required periodic meetings

with specialists to develop and monitor Jordy's education plan, which outlined things Mom must do each day in addition to the regular chores of parenting and housekeeping. Maybe you can relate to this situation.

Sometimes, fatigue leads to frustration, which may be directed toward other family members, or even the child. This added to Jordy's parents' physical, emotional, and spiritual exhaustion. Anxiety also surfaced in regard to Jordy's and the family's future. Time was always in short supply. But "time" is not something we own, not something we can "add."

Just because your life seems harder than that of your friends who are not dealing with disability does not mean life is "bad" in the sense of being inferior or terrible. It only means your life is different. The difficulty and stress you feel is simply different from that of families not affected by disability.

David's words in Psalm 37 remind us our relationship with God is critical, and tell us what we need to do: Trust in the Lord. Delight in the Lord. Commit your ways to the Lord. Rest in the Lord. Feed on his faithfulness. This is the reason for the trust David instructs us to have: God *is* faithful. His faithfulness does not depend on us; we trust and rest in him, and feed on his faithfulness.

Fretting over the demands and responsibilities of raising a child who is disabled only increases your apprehension and uncertainty. To delight in the Lord is for your spirit to rest in him, recognizing his many blessings and clinging to his promises.

To commit your way to the Lord includes giving over to him your desires and your burdens, trusting that where he leads is better than where you go by yourself. It acknowledges that his wisdom and ways are far superior to your own yearnings; that God will work all things together for good for those who love him. To rest in the Lord is to be surrendered to him; to be still, knowing that he is God (Psalm 46:10).

FOR REFLECTION

Romans 8:28 is another oft-quoted passage. Reflect on this teaching in terms of God's presence as you struggle with issues of disability. Let them help you "slow down" so you can appreciate God's presence and faithfulness.

TAKE ACTION

In Psalm 16:11 David praises God: "You make known to me the path of life; in your presence there is fullness of joy; at your right hand are pleasures forevermore." Your busyness will continue, but though you grow weary, bask in the Lord and receive his joy. Slow down; take time to appreciate your child. Stay grounded in the Lord; rest in God's faithfulness.

DAY 32

SORROWFUL OR CHEERFUL HEART? TRUSTING IN GOD'S FUTURE GRACE

"A glad heart makes a cheerful face, but by sorrow of heart the spirit is crushed. … All the days of the afflicted are evil, but the cheerful of heart has a continual feast." (Proverbs 15:13, 15b)

"Do not be anxious, saying, 'What shall we eat?' or 'What shall we drink?' or 'What shall we wear?' For the Gentiles seek after all these things, and your heavenly Father knows that you need them all. But seek first the kingdom of God and his righteousness, and all these things will be added to you. Therefore do not be anxious about tomorrow, for tomorrow will be anxious for itself." (Matthew 6:31-34a)

Dealing with disability naturally draws attention to your present circumstances. But this limits your perspective and increases sorrow. Your focus must be on God and his promises.

The verses from Proverbs 15 focus on the heart and the contrast between joy and depression. Our face often betrays our emotions. A "cheerful face" implies a cheerful heart, one that is full of joy despite circumstances. It signals a pleasing relationship with God. Proverbs 15:15 refers to the days of the afflicted as "evil," meaning they are troubling or distressing, producing anxiety. But considering things (like disability) troubling depends on your point of view. Circumstances of life are beyond our control but we can control our heart-attitude. A cheerful heart is one which is unruffled and quiet. The person whose heart is at peace despite life's circumstances has a "continual feast" because they are able to overcome their anxious thoughts. The key to having joy in your heart is to see your experience from God's perspective. Jesus helps us see this in Matthew 6:25-34.

The full Matthew passage is probably familiar, but you may not have connected it to disability. Jesus says God's will and righteousness should be your top priority. God knows and will take care of your needs. Worrying about what *tomorrow* will bring for you or your disabled loved one leads to a loss of joy for *today*.

Jesus pointed to God's extravagant care for birds, lilies, and field grass and asked "Will God not also have great care for humankind?" Since God knows your needs, cares, and concerns Jesus urged relaxing and focusing on God and his righteousness. God's care is constant and unending. As a believer, you have a favored relationship with God giving assurance of his unmeasured and ongoing grace — for you and your disabled loved one.

The picture Jesus painted illustrates and guarantees God's care for his creation. Birds, lilies, and grass are relatively insignificant, yet God cares for them. People who are disabled may be seen by some as insignificant, but God sees beauty in them and cares for them. God will graciously provide for your needs and the needs of your disabled loved one. Putting God's will and God's righteousness first is your life is critical; God will take care of the everyday things.

Don't waste time thinking about the unchangeable past ("if only") or the unknown future ("what if"). Faith involves trusting God even without knowing what he is doing or where he is leading. And don't feel guilty about being overcome with grief or anxiety, or directing your complaints toward God. He is stronger than your grief and is pleased when you lay your heart bare before him. God, the giver of grace, does not change according to your experiences. Trust God, not just for his past act of saving grace, but also for his future grace, his ongoing care and unfailing love.

FOR REFLECTION

"The cheerful of heart has a continual feast." Read Luke 14:12-24 where Jesus talks about the Great Banquet. Note who are brought to the feast after those originally invited refused to come. How does thinking that your disabled loved one is a special and desired guest at God's banquet table help you to "see" God's future grace?

TAKE ACTION

In Colossians 2:7 Paul urges believers to abound in thanksgiving. Thanksgiving implies that your heart is happy or cheerful regardless of the circumstances of life which, for the present moment may appear negative. How can you keep your heart "cheerful" and focused on God?

DAY 33

GOD'S VISION FOR THE DISABLED

*"Blessed are you who weep now, for
you shall laugh." (Luke 6:21b)*

*"I consider that the sufferings of this present time are
not worth comparing with the glory that is to be revealed
to us. ... For the creation was subjected to futility,
not willingly, but because of him who subjected it, in
hope that the creation itself will be set free from its
bondage to corruption and obtain the freedom of the
glory of the children of God." (Romans 8:18, 20-21)*

*"Strengthen the weak hands, and make firm the feeble
knees. Say to those who have an anxious heart, 'Be strong;
fear not! Behold, your God will come with vengeance, with
the recompense of God. He will come and save you.' Then
the eyes of the blind shall be opened, and the ears of the
deaf unstopped; then shall the lame man leap like a deer,
and the tongue of the mute sing for joy." (Isaiah 35:3-6a)*

*"They who wait for the LORD shall renew their
strength; they shall mount up with wings like
eagles; they shall run and not be weary; they
shall walk and not faint." (Isaiah 40:31)*

If your family is like others affected by disability you know how easily you become nearsighted, focusing on issues surrounding impairment. Centering on present needs fuels distress and weeping, but God promises a future filled with laughter.

Romans 8 explains that our first parents put personal interests ahead of Godly obedience, resulting in creation being subjected to futility and frustration. Creation became *abnormal,* allowing disability to become a normal part of life. We're all subject to illness, accidents, and the effects of aging. All creation groans but, in hope, awaits Christ's return.

God's vision, unlike ours, is not limited to what is seen now. Isaiah 35 and 40 provide a glimpse into God's unlimited vision by picturing complete restoration when Christ's kingdom is established. The prophet speaks of future joy and comfort for God's people when disability is ended and everything returns to the perfect, Edenic state. Jesus' earthly ministry previewed the prophecy's fulfillment as he restored many to fellowship in the community by giving sight to some who were blind, enabled some who were deaf and mute to hear and speak, and gave physical strength to others. These miracles verified Jesus' claim to be God's Son and foreshadowed what will be for all who trust in him in the new heaven and earth, where disability will, at most, be only a distant memory. For all who hope in the Lord, there will be renewal.

As God's vision for the future becomes reality, the groaning will cease and rejoicing commence because the curse is lifted (Romans 8). For people dealing with issues of disability, this message of hope anticipates a future when disability will be no more. But your disabled loved one does not have to wait until that future time to have joy and peace in the Lord, nor should they feel they have nothing to offer the community of faith. Few people are aware that the familiar hymn "Just as I am, without one plea but that thy blood was shed for me" was written by Charlotte Elliot, a woman with poor health and in frequent pain. Despite a severe illness resulting in permanent disability, she knew she was loved and accepted by God *just as she was.* Her hymn has contributed to the spiritual journey of many.

Still have doubts? Know that God is working behind the scenes.

Don't be anxious; don't wrestle with yourself and your situation. Trust God; rest in his wisdom and goodness. God has promised his presence, unfailing love, and provision. Though we are often inconsistent, Jesus never changes.

FOR REFLECTION

Meditate on Hebrews 12:1-2. Fix your eyes of Jesus, the founder and perfecter of our faith. What you presently endure pales in comparison to what Jesus endured on the cross. Draw strength from him.

TAKE ACTION

1 Corinthians 13:12 says "Now we see in a mirror dimly, but then face to face. Now I know in part; then I shall know fully, even as I have been fully known." Without clear vision it is easy to be trapped in your life with disability and lose sight of the hope we have in Christ. What helps you maintain your focus on Christ? How can you help your disabled family member see God's love and promises?

DAY 34

BE STILL, AND KNOW

"Be still, and know that I am God. I will be exalted among the nations, I will be exalted in the earth!" (Psalm 46:10)

Yesterday's devotional began with reference to Jesus' words, "Blessed are you who weep now, for you shall laugh" (Luke 6:21), and a reminder of how easy it is to become overly focused on the impact of your own or your loved one's disability. Psalm 46 also gives direction on handling the day-to-day responsibilities which have the potential to overwhelm our lives.

Psalm 46 begins by declaring God to be a refuge and strength, a helper who is always present. We readily acknowledge God's presence when thing are going well, but the psalm reminds us that he is also present in times of outward distress (the earth giving way, the waters roaring, the mountains crumbling), and times of inner turmoil when we feel drained of physical and emotional strength and our lives seem thrown into disorder. Depending on the specific needs of a disabled family member, this disarray may seem a daily experience.

Having a family member who is disabled can complicate an already overly-taxed life. At such times, the words of Psalm 46:10 are important to remember: Be still; know that God *is* God. Though we change, God remains constant and consistent. The Hebrew word translated "still" means to stop striving to do things in your own strength, to relax. Recall times when you found relaxation and renewal by bathing in warm water. God wants us to bathe in the knowledge of who he is and of his intense and never-changing love. Being still means relinquishing the driver's seat and letting God manage your life.

This does not mean a lessening of daily responsibilities to meet the needs of your disabled loved one, but it does mean remaining confident that God is in charge. He knows your needs and the limitations of your ability. His strength is not limited, nor does it fluctuate. Verse 1 of the psalm says God is our refuge — a shelter or strong rock in times of storm. In verses 7 and 11, God is described as our fortress — an unassailable stronghold which cannot be breeched. The only thing that can interfere with God's guiding, assisting, or defending us as his children is our insistence on being in control of our lives. Hence, we are urged to be "still and know" that God is God, that he will be exalted among the nations — and in our lives. God is a safe place of refuge, always ready to come to our assistance.

Often, people with a disability display "stillness" before God more easily that people who are able-bodied. Young Elliot, the boy with cerebral palsy mentioned in an earlier devotional (day 9), displays a fearlessness that some might think rash. But his quickness to enter into a new situation is better understood as trusting, being "still" and knowing that God is with him. The eagerness with which Elliot seeks to experience the world, and the quickness of his response to engage in worship is a simple example of the attitude which the psalmist advocates.

FOR REFLECTION

Perhaps you can relate to the feelings expressed in Psalm 42 of panting, thirsting, and crying after God. Have there been times who you asked, "Where are you, God?" But the author of Psalm

42 goes on to rebuke himself, asking "why am I so discouraged, why is my heart in turmoil?" He reminds himself to hope in God and to praise God. This response came as the psalmist shifted his focus from his circumstances to God, whom he describes as his Rock (42:9). How has God been your "rock" of refuge and security?

TAKE ACTION

Psalm 46:8 invites us to marvel at the works of the Lord and refers to God's actions on behalf of Israel. We must learn to "see" God's glorious works in our lives and families. What examples of God's presence and provision in your life, and that of your disabled loved one, can you focus on right now that will lead you to be still and know, experientially and emotionally, that God is God?

DAY 35

THE BLESSING OF FRIENDSHIP

*"You are my friends if you do what I command you.
No longer do I call you servants, for the servant does
not know what his master is doing; but I have called
you friends, for all that I have heard from my Father
I have made known to you." (John 15:14–15)*

*"And behold, I am with you always, to the
end of the age." (Matthew 28:20b)*

*"Let us consider how to stir up one another to love and
good works, not neglecting to meet together, as is the habit
of some, but encouraging one another" (Hebrews 10:24-25)*

Do you ever feel alone? Are there days when the necessity of caring for a child or family member with a disability demands more energy and time than you feel you have to offer? For many of my friends in Kenya who have a child who is disabled, this might be a "normal" day. In many cases, the children's father has absented himself from the family because one of the children has a disability, usually blaming the wife for the child's disability. Often the extended family has no real involvement or apparent concern for the mom and her children. There is little government assistance for the family, nor are social or medical services readily available. But even if these were options, the absence of loving relationships still remains. These factors contribute to feelings of loneliness and discouragement.

Jesus' words in John 15:15, "I call you friends," bring encouragement and comfort through knowing we are never truly alone. Jesus' friendship never ceases. Earthly friends, even Christian brothers and sisters, and not always available when we need them. But Jesus is always ready to fellowship with us. In difficult or discouraging times you may feel alone and wonder if Jesus has left you. It is not Jesus who has "moved," but you. Jesus promised in Matthew 28:20 never to leave us, and, as children of God, we know we will be with him forever. Fellowship with other believers, especially those who also deal with issues of disability and can relate to your struggles, is valuable. But knowing that Jesus is a friend who is always present is even more precious.

In the original Greek, the words of Jesus in John 15:15 are strong and personal: *you* have I *named* my friends. Naming us his friends creates a relationship which revolves around Jesus' love for us, our love for him, and our love for one another. It also entails obedience (doing what he commands; John 15:14, 17), and fruitfulness (John 15:16). The proof of our love for Jesus is not in how we feel, but in our actions.

God's call is not just to friendship and fellowship with him, but with one another. This fellowship is grounded in the life of God, who is the source of both our physical and spiritual life. The closeness of our fellowship with other believers allows us to mutually share our felt needs and concerns. But if seeking assistance or solace from others is our primary reason for fellowship, it fails to display the element of love and true friendship. Our deepest need, especially in times of struggle and weariness from dealing with issues related to disability, is for God, who invites us to find rest in him. God has blessed us with his friendship, and has charged us to be friends with one another. The author of Hebrews urged us to consider how we can motivate each other to love and good works, to meet with and encourage one another. Sometimes the best approach to handling our difficulties is to help others who face similar trials.

FOR REFLECTION

What does being a friend to others mean to you? How have you found deep fellowship with others who face struggles associated with disability? How has God given you hope and encouragement through your relationship with others? How has God enabled you to provide friendly fellowship with others? How has your disabled child or family member encouraged you?

TAKE ACTION

Read Romans 12:6–8 and 1 Corinthians 12:4–11 where Paul speaks about gifts which God has given believers. Paul says God has given every believer, including those with a disability, at least one spiritual gift. The gifts identified in these passages are not identical, suggesting that Paul did not identify every gift, but was listing categories of gifts. What gift has God given you to enable you to be a friend to others, to give encouragement and care as needed?

Friendship among believers is also a gift from God, but it does not require face to face communication. My friends in Kenya, though living in different towns and without ease of travel, regularly check in with one another via cell phone, and mutually bask in their friendship. Would this work for you as well?

DAY 36

NO ORDINARY CHILD

"Now a man from the house of Levi went and took as his wife a Levite woman. The woman conceived and bore a son, and when she saw that he was a fine child, she hid him three months. When she could hide him no longer, she took for him a basket made of bulrushes and daubed it with bitumen [tar] and pitch. She put the child in it and placed it among the reeds by the river bank. And his sister stood at a distance to know what would be done to him. Now the daughter of Pharaoh came down to bathe at the river . . . She saw the basket among the reeds . . . and she took it. When she opened it, she saw the child, and behold, the baby was crying. She took pity on him and said, "This is one of the Hebrews' children." (Exodus 2:1–6)

"By faith Moses, when he was born, was hidden for three months by his parents, because they saw that the child was beautiful, and they were not afraid of the king's edict." (Hebrews 11:2)

During the months of pregnancy, expectant parents often fantasize about what their child will be like, what joy he or she might bring to the family. As the expected due-date draws closer, a sense of anticipation, perhaps mixed with a tinge of apprehension, grows. Moses' mother surely had concerns during her pregnancy, especially knowing that Pharaoh had ordered that every male child born to a Hebrew mother be cast into the Nile (Exodus 1:22). After courageously hiding him for three months, she prepared a specially made basket to hold Moses and placed it among the reeds on the banks of the Nile. The Bible says she did this because she saw that Moses was a "fine" child. The Hebrew word used to describe the baby is *tobe,* which can be translated good, beautiful, or special. The author of Hebrews wrote that Moses as "no ordinary child" (NIV).

Was it just physical handsomeness or health that his mother saw in Moses? Did she sense that God had some special purpose in mind for him? Did she think God might use him to bring an end to the Hebrews' slavery in Egypt? The Bible gives no insight into her thinking, but does attest to her faith in God and, indeed, God did use the baby to touch the heart of Pharaoh's daughter.

Malaika's beginning was less favorable than Moses'. Born with Down syndrome, her birth-mother saw no beauty or specialness in her, and abandoned her by the side of the road, as one might do with unwanted trash. Perhaps she feared rejection by her family and community, or perhaps assumed that personal sin or a family curse resulted in Malaika's condition. If you have a child with a disability you, too, may have experienced negativity from others, or wondered if you had done something that led to your child's disability.

Just as Moses' story turned out well, so has Malaika's. A compassionate person "rescued" her from the trash heap, as it were, and brought her to Eva. Eva confirmed the diagnosis of Down syndrome but, rather than seeing a person of no value, she saw Malaika's beauty and eventually adopted her. Eva's training in special education and her Christian faith resulted in Malaika's being nourished, both physically and spiritually. Today, Malaika is an energetic child enrolled in an inclusive school program whose teachers also recognize her beauty and believe in her potential. Malaika has been a blessing to her adoptive family and to others who get to know her.

FOR REFLECTION

When you look at your disabled child, what do you see? Do you, like Moses' mother, see your child as "fine" and "beautiful"? The diagnostic label placed on a child often causes people to focus on limitation rather than possibility. How can you remain focused on the positive "specialness" of your child, on how your child is a blessing to you and the whole family?

We know from Scripture what God accomplished through Moses despite his speech impediment (Exodus 4:10). Imagine how God may use your child, regardless of his or her disability, to bless your family and others.

TAKE ACTION

Psalm 127:3 says "children are a heritage from the Lord, the fruit of the womb a reward." The psalmist does not qualify this statement in a way that only healthy and non-disabled children are in view. The way the verse is translated by Peterson brings home the point: "Don't you see that children are God's best gift? The fruit of the womb his generous legacy?" (MSG). What does it take for you to recognize this in your child? Keep a daily journal of reflections on how your child is revealed to be God's best gift to you.

DAY 37

SABBATH REST

*"Come to me, all who labor and are heavy laden,
and I will give you rest. Take my yoke upon you, and
learn from me, for I am gentle and lowly in heart,
and you will find rest for your souls. For my yoke is
easy, and my burden is light." (Matthew 11:28–30)*

*"Thus says the LORD: "Stand by the roads, and look,
and ask for the ancient paths, where the good way is; and
walk in it, and find rest for your souls." (Jeremiah 6:16)*

"Be still, and know that I am God." (Psalm 46:10a)

Being the parent or spouse of someone with a significant disability can be very tiring and there may be few times to simply relax. Disability does not take a day off and, depending on family resources and available help from friends, there may be little "down time" for the primary caregiver. "Rest" can become a shattered or illusory expectation.

The words of Jesus in Matthew 11 were specifically given in the context of the Jewish people being overburdened by the legalistic demands of the Pharisees. Jesus' words echo those of Jeremiah where God promises rest to those who turn to him. "Sabbath rest" is something which God wants for all his people. We err if we restrict Sabbath rest to mean Sunday only. Rather, Sabbath rest is a way of being — an inner peace that can only be found as we ground ourselves in him as our source of life and spiritual nourishment. We often associate "Sabbath" with the seventh day, as in Genesis

2:2–3 which tells us that God rested from the work of creation on the seventh day. But the "Sabbath" refers to ceasing from labor, not to a day of the week. God "rested" because the work of creating was completed, but he did not stop sustaining the world.

Even so, the physical "labor" of caring for someone continues, and depending on the type and degree of disability may be life-long. The rest that Jesus offers is not vacation time, but a stillness, and inner tranquility that comes from knowing him. This changes the way we look at the responsibilities and requirements of being a caregiver. Jesus knows our struggles and lovingly calls us to cast our cares on him, our source of rest and refreshment. His words reflect his gentle nature as he calls us to be "yoked" with him as an unfailing companion in our daily walk, making our burdens "light."

Often, our disabled loved one becomes a physical example of what it means to "rest," to be still in Jesus. Sandra is a young girl with severe cerebral palsy. Her quadriplegia leaves her completely dependent on others for her daily care: dressing, feeding, toileting, and moving her from room to room in her wheelchair. Her only way of communicating is through her beautiful smile and bright eyes, which reveal her awareness, intelligence, and pleasure at being in the company of others. She sits in silence and vulnerability, appreciating the blessings of others — and blessing them in return through her unspoken display of love and grace. If our eyes are open, if we are looking for Jesus, we need look no further than Sandra to be reminded of his love and his care, and to find rest in him. Sandra is a visible representation of God's invitation in Psalm 46:10 "be still, and know that he is God."

FOR REFLECTION

Psalm 91:1 says "He who dwells in the shelter of the Most High will abide in the shadow of the Almighty." This creates an image of a mother bird cradling her chicks under her wings, which suggests a complete resting trust on the part of the chicks. The psalmist continues in verse 2, "I will say to the LORD, 'My refuge and my fortress, my God, in whom I trust.'" Here, God is likened to a place of shelter and safety, suggesting protections from physical enemies. But God's ability to shelter us applies equally to safety from the "enemies" of time, which often seems in short supply, and of necessity, the tyranny of the urgent. The words of Jesus in Matthew 11 seem to echo the ideas expressed by the psalmist. In the midst of the daily busyness of caring for your disabled child or family member, how can you remember Jesus' call to find rest in him — to welcome and rely on his presence and strength as you love and serve your family? What visible reminders of resting in Jesus can you place around the house to keep you spiritually and emotionally "rested"?

DAY 38

ALL THINGS WORK TOGETHER FOR GOOD

"And we know that for those who love God all things work together for good, for those who are called according to his purpose. For those whom he foreknew he also predestined to be conformed to the image of his Son, in order that he might be the firstborn among many brothers." (Romans 8:28–29)

Paul's words in Romans 8:28–39 are beloved to all Christians. But when a child is born with a disability or a family member become disabled through accident or illness, a person's faith may be challenged. Has God turned away? Have I done, or failed to do, something that has brought God's judgment in the form of a disability?

These verses in Romans do not promise a life free of troubles or trials, or that God will allow only "good" things in our life. The word "good" that Paul uses means useful or beneficial. Paul assures us that God is able to work every detail of the lives of those who love him into something good. Though we may not perceive specific happenings as "good," God can use them in a way that the ultimate good results: our conformity to the image of Christ. God's goal is to shape our lives to be like Jesus, but we must remember that Jesus' earthly life was not without tribulation. Just as Jesus' suffering brought about good, so God can bring good into and through our life regardless of our ability or disability. In fact, our ability can sometimes get in God's way! Paul's positive outlook is succinctly captured in this paraphrase: "God knew what he was doing from the very beginning. He decided from the outset to shape the lives of those who love him along the same lines as the life of his Son" (MSG).

Greg and Jelena have been blessed with three beautiful children, the youngest of whom, Hana, has autism. God used Hana to move Greg and Jelena into ministry to individuals and families who deal with disability. As a result of their ministry, many families have changed how they see their disabled offspring, and how they see God. Nevertheless, Greg and Jelena still face struggles as they love and care for Hana. As does every parent, Jelena wonders what each day will bring in Hana's life. Even more worrisome is what each day will *not* bring. What will Hana *not* be successful at today that would be no challenge to a child without autism?

God's promise cannot be voided by disability. No disabling condition is stronger than God. Concern for a family member who is disabled reflects our love, but we become shortsighted if we take our eyes off God's goodness and his ability to take what we see as bad or undesirable and bring good out of it.

To say God "foreknew" us expresses God's intimate knowledge and love, a love which is goal-oriented: our conformity to the image of Christ. This reshaping begins when Christ enters our lives and continues daily. Life events, whether positive or negative, work into the process of change. The difficulty for us is trusting that God can bring good out of what we perceive as bad.

Can a person with autism or other intellectual disability be conformed to the image of Christ? What was the shape of Jesus' life? The gospels clearly show Jesus as loving, gentle, patient, and accepting of others. People with significant disabilities sometimes more readily display these qualities than those who are able-bodied. Like us, they can become angry or impatient, but they also can more quickly lose that negativity, and can more readily forgive our hasty actions or words. Hana and others with a disability share the vulnerability of Jesus, who chose to make himself vulnerable, even unto death (Philippians 2:5–8).

Paul wants us to understand that what happens in our lives serves a purpose. God has a reason for allowing things we find undesirable to enter our lives, even disability. God is not required to explain what he is doing or allowing in our life; our obligation is to trust and follow wherever and however he leads.

FOR REFLECTION

In John 14:27, Jesus said, "Peace I leave with you; my peace I give to you. . . Let not your hearts be troubled, neither let them be afraid." Trusting, and resting in the peace which Jesus gives, is sometimes difficult when we have a child or other family member who is disabled. Watching them struggle through life "hurts." How can you "rest" in the peace that Jesus gives?

TAKE ACTION

List ways in which your disabled loved one shows he or she is being shaped to be like Christ, and give thanks for what God is doing. Then list ways in which your disabled family member has helped *you* to grow in Christlikeness.

DAY 39

INSEPARABLE LOVE OF GOD

"If God is for us, who can be against us? . . . . Who shall separate us from the love of Christ? Shall tribulation, or distress, or persecution, or famine, or nakedness, or danger, or sword? . . . . No, in all these things we are more than conquerors through him who loved us. For I am sure that neither death nor life, nor angels nor rulers, nor things present nor things to come, nor powers, nor height nor depth, nor anything else in all creation, will be able to separate us from the love of God in Christ Jesus our Lord." (Romans 8:31b, 35, 37–39)

The previous devotional focused on God's ability to work things together for good, clearly asserting that all "things" are under God's control. Paul takes this theological truth a step further in today's passage, arguing that there is nothing which can separate us from the love of Christ. He gives an extensive list of things that are incapable of separating us from the love of God in Christ. Extrinsic events like tribulation, distress, persecution, famine, nakedness, danger, or sword are not strong enough to disconnect us from God, but neither can death or life, angels, or rulers. So great is the depth of God's love that Paul adds there is nothing present or future, nor *anything else in all creation* which can separate us from God's love in Christ Jesus. Though Paul does not specifically include disability is his list, it certainly comes under the category of "anything else in creation." None of the things Paul mentions are stronger than God's love. God may allow us to experience various trials, but they do not prevent his love.

Some people mistakenly believe that becoming disabled or giving birth to a child with a disability signifies God's displeasure or the removal of his love. There is no biblical basis for this claim, and I believe Paul would be quick to deny its validity. Caring for a child who has a disability can seem like a lonely and wearisome job. Facing the same struggles each day but seeing little progress can exhaust a person's physical, emotional, and spiritual energy. Time spent caring for a child with significant disabilities may also disrupt relationships with friends, leaving parents feeling lost and alone as they strive to meet the child's needs, promote his or her development, and keep up with daily responsibilities. Though all children pass through the same developmental stages, for a child who has a disability, these stages are often delayed or prolonged.

When you feel overburdened, remember what Paul said: if God is for us, who can be against us? With God on our side, how can we lose?

Lyuda, a woman I met Ukraine, was formerly the wife of a colonel in the army. One day while on a ladder picking fruit from a tree, she spotted a toddler making his way toward the stream flowing behind her house. In her haste to reach the boy lest he fall into the water, she fell from the ladder. Her back was broken, leaving her a paraplegic. Soon thereafter, her husband divorced her, perhaps thinking she was no longer of value to him. Many who find themselves in a similar situation would be angry with God for allowing the accident. They might argue that Paul was mistaken, claiming that either the disability separated her from God's love or God, for some unknown reason, removed his love, allowing her to become disabled. But God's actions are not arbitrary (and he is not obligated to explain his actions to us), and we can be certain that there is nothing we can do to cancel his love for his own.

Lyuda now lives in an accessible building in a comfortable

apartment that accommodates her wheelchair. She has become the primary caregiver for her young grandson who, along with her confidence in God's ongoing love, brightens her days. Lyuda is a believer and has a most contagious smile and voices a strong testimony to those who ask how she can have peace and joy despite her need for a wheelchair. In many ways, Lyuda is more than a conqueror, inseparable from the love of God in Christ Jesus her Lord. She readily confesses that God is able to work all things together for good.

FOR REFLECTION

How do the words of Joshua 1:5 and Hebrews 13:5, which speak of God's never leaving or forsaking us, connect with Paul's teaching in Romans 8?

In 2 Corinthians 4:7–9, Paul compares us to fragile jars. But being a "broken pot" does not separate us from the love of God in Christ Jesus. In our brokenness we better appreciate God's inseparable love, and through our brokenness, God is able to bring glory to himself.

TAKE ACTION

Paul's words in Romans 8 assure us of God's ongoing love and, by implication, of his sovereignty. Take time each day to reflect on the ways in which you have seen God's love for you and your disabled family member — perhaps even seen God's love *through* that individual. List them, and praise God for his love.

DAY 40

GOD'S ABUNDANT GOODNESS

"Oh, how abundant is your goodness, which you have stored up for those who fear you and worked for those who take refuge in you, in the sight of the children of mankind! . . . . Be strong, and let your heart take courage, all you who wait for the LORD!" (Psalm 31:19, 34)

David begins this psalm by declaring that he takes refuge in God, calling God a rock of refuge and a strong fortress. Clearly, his trust is in God, not in himself. The psalm was probably written around the time of his son, Absalom's, rebellion, when even David's trusted counselor, Ahithophel, had deserted him to follow Absalom (2 Samuel 15–18).

Having worked with families affected by disability, I know that they can easily relate to David's description of his circumstances: distressed and grieved (v. 9); his life consumed with sorrow (v. 10); a reproach to his neighbors (v. 11); forgotten like a broken vessel (v. 12); shamed (v. 17); cut off from God's sight (v. 22). Perhaps there are times when you would echo David's words. Sometimes relationships with close relatives or friends cool, and people become more distant emotionally. Sometimes, wrong theology leads others to become critical and judgmental towards you and your situation. Sometimes caring for your disabled family member is so time consuming that you don't have the energy to maintain relationships. Sometimes you may feel forgotten and cut off, not just from friends and family, but from God. Sometimes, you may feel that disability is an enemy from which you need to appeal to God for deliverance.

But disability is not your enemy; in fact, for some it has become a blessing. Joni Eareckson Tada has been a quadriplegic for 50 years, but confesses that she would rather be in her wheelchair and have a personal relationship with God than be able-bodied, but without him in her life. God has truly blessed Joni, and through the ministry of Joni and Friends many thousands of others — with and without disabilities — have been blessed.

David's laments, however, are countered by his words of trust in God and the steadfastness of God's love (vv. 6–7, 14). He knows that his times are in God's hands (v. 15) and that God will not leave him in a state of anxiety or confusion (v. 17). He exults is God's abundant goodness which is lavished on all who revere God and seek refuge in him. God's goodness and love were all that David needed. And they are all we need as we deal with issues of disability and people's attitude.

David lost any sense of discouragement or confusion when he remembered the goodness of God that is freely given to him. Similarly, any confusion of loneliness you feel in your "battle" with disability can be conquered through trusting and resting in the Lord, confident in his promise of abundant blessing being yours through Christ. The goodness of God is not just stored for the future, but is available to you now. Draw courage and strength from the Lord to help you through the trials of this life. But as David did, be certain to give God the glory.

FOR REFLECTION

People often make the mistake of interpreting scripture by their experiences and situation. Rather, we must let scripture interpret our experience. Knowing God is in control and that his love and goodness do not change, what do you need to do to draw closer to him when you struggle to understand life events?

Meditate on Psalm 17:6–8. Make a list of ways that God has shown you the wonders of his love. Do you recognize that you are the apple of God's eye? That he keeps you in the shadow of his wings? How does that empower you as you face the daily challenges of disability?

CONCLUDING THOUGHTS

The title of this book is "Forty Days: Finding Refuge in the Ark from the Storms of Disability." That title may bring to mind the story of Noah. But the focus of Day 40's devotional was King David's finding refuge in God, not a boat. God, of course, was the real refuge for Noah and his family, too. After all, it was God who warned Noah of the impending judgment, it was God who gave the blueprint for the ark's construction, and it was God who brought the animals, told Noah to get in, and closed the door.

Finding refuge in the "ark" that is God, is something that we all need. It is my prayer that all who read these devotional studies gain strength, comfort, and peace from God, our Savior and Lord.

SUGGESTIONS FOR FURTHER READING

Hubach, Stephanie O. (2006). *Same lake, different boat: Coming alongside people touched by disability.* Phillipsburg, NJ: P & R Publishing.

Bradley, Lorna (2015). *Special needs parenting: From coping to thriving.* Minneapolis, MN: Huff Publishing Associates.

Linder, Beverly (2010). *A never-give-up heart: Pursuing God's design for the special-needs family.* Colorado Springs, CO: Special Heart.

Linder, Beverly (2014). *Un-special needs: There's more to your child than "special needs."* Colorado Springs, CO: Special Heart.

Wilson, Andrew & Wilson, Rachel (2016). *The life we never expected.* Wheaton, IL: Crossway.

Tada, Joni Eareckson (2009). *A lifetime of wisdom: Embracing the way God heals you.* Grand Rapids, MI: Zondervan.

Tada, Joni Eareckson & Estes, Steve (2001). *A step further: Growing closer to God through hurt and hardship.* Grand Rapids, MI: Zondervan.

Joni and Friends (2017). *Real families, real needs: A compassionate guide for families living with disability.* Carol Stream, IL: Tyndale House.

Mazza, Doug & Bundy, Steve (2014). *Another kind of courage: God's design for fathers of families affected by disability.* Agoura Hills, CA: Joni and Friends

Philo, Jolene (2011). *Different dream parenting: A practical guide to raising a child with special needs.* Grand Rapids, MI: Discovery House.

Printed in the United States
By Bookmasters